DISCARDED

JUL 1 6 2025

How to

Illustrations by Charles Bragg

PETER PASSELL

How to

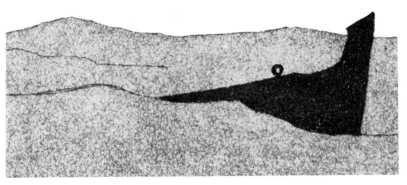

Farrar, Straus and Giroux · *New York*

Copyright © 1976 by Peter Passell
Illustrations copyright © 1972, 1973, 1974, 1976
by Charles Bragg
All rights reserved
Printed in the United States of America
Published simultaneously in Canada
by McGraw-Hill Ryerson Ltd., Toronto
Designed by Marion Hess

Portions of the text originally appeared in *Playboy*.

Library of Congress Cataloging in Publication Data
Passell, Peter.
How to.
Includes index.
1. Handbooks, vade-mecums, etc.   I. Title.
AG105.P25   031'.02   75-34444

How to

HOW TO AVOID SHARK BITE

ANever underestimate the power of the press. Since the release of *Jaws*, shark attack has vaulted from the number thirty-six position in popular fears (just behind ring around the collar) to number eleven (tied with mixed marriage). Even the sharks seem to have caught the spirit. Sightings near beaches have doubled in the past year, though many reports are inaccurate. The brave burghers of Miami Beach, for example, bludgeoned to death one ten-foot invader, only to discover the victim was a baby whale.

Still, better safe than sorry. For those who wish to be prepared, here's the latest on how to preserve life and limb.

Elude 'em. Sharks don't have anything particular against humans; they are much too dumb to hold grudges. The going theory, these days, is that aggressive shark species eat everything that is accessible. The more you resemble easy prey, the more likely you are to get eaten. Hence the obvious precautions. Avoid swimming near concentrations of fish—natural bait for sharks. Avoid dead fish in the water—sharks have good noses. Avoid high-contrast clothing—sharks perceive contrast better than color. Don't splash about near sharks—it reminds them of wounded fish.

On the other hand, don't believe the myth that you're safe swimming in cold water. Few shark attacks have been recorded in water below 65 degrees because few people swim in water below 65 degrees. Shallow water offers little protection if it is close to a deep channel.

Repel 'em. Chemical shark repellents don't work very well. The U.S. Navy uses something called Shark Chaser, a mixture of copper acetate and black dye, developed during World War II. The copper acetate supposedly reduces shark appetite, while the dye hides the potential victim. Unfortunately, the combination hasn't proved effective outside the laboratory.

What does work is a simple camouflage device called the Shark Screen. This is nothing more than a dull-colored plastic sack with a flotation collar, big enough for a person to fit inside. Sharks ignore it because it doesn't resemble an ordinary meal. And unlike Shark Chaser, the protection lasts indefinitely.

Kill 'em. The standard anti-shark weapon for divers is

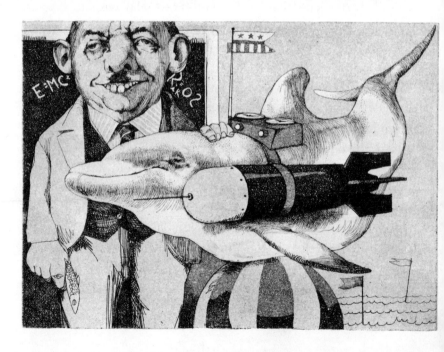

the bang stick. It's just a long pole with a shotgun shell and trigger device on the business end. Unfortunately (as everybody who saw the movie knows), the bang stick will stop a big shark only if you nail the beast directly in the brain. Sharks have very small brains.

Other weapons may revolutionize the art. The Shark Dart, carried by Navy divers at Apollo splashdowns, punctures the skin with a hollow steel needle, then fills up the shark's gut with compressed gas. Very deadly. An electric dart, also being tested by the Navy, paralyzes the monster with a thirty-volt shock. Disadvantage: when the battery wears out, so does the paralysis.

Probably the most appealing anti-shark weapon under development, though, is the porpoise. Porpoises defend their young by ramming predators at high velocity with their thick skulls. The Navy hopes to train them to do the same on behalf of divers. A big problem is getting porpoises angry enough to risk their own hides.

Eat 'em. Should you tangle with a shark and win, the following recipe will come in handy:

SHARK À LA ROSS

    2 lbs. filets from young, medium-sized shark,
       preferably a Mako (no dark meat)
    2 shallots, chopped
    ½ cup parsley, chopped
    ¼ cup fresh basil, chopped
    ¼ cup dry white wine
    ¼ cup fish stock
    4 tbs. butter
    ½ lemon
    salt and white pepper

Sprinkle the bottom of a buttered baking dish with the shallots, parsley, and basil. Pour in the wine and stock. Rub both sides of the filets with salt and pepper; place in the baking dish. Squeeze lemon juice over the fish and dot with butter.

Cook, uncovered, in a preheated 350-degree oven for 20 minutes, basting a few times with the pan liquid. Then brown under the broiler for a minute. Garnish with parsley sprigs and lemon wedges.

Serves 6.

HOW TO BEAT A HANGOVER

BYou know what a hangover is, we know what a hangover is. The only people who don't are the researchers the federal government pays to figure out a cure for it.

The hangover, it seems, is a great mystery. Alcohol is not a healthy beverage—the stuff rots brain cells and scars the liver. None of this, however, explains why you feel lousy the next morning. A number of theories, lightly buoyed by facts, are floating around these days, and each suggests a different tack.

The overexertion theory. Drinking is fun because it anesthetizes the parts of the brain in charge of saying no. Inhibitions disappear, and along with them goes the com-

mon sense to quit when you are fatigued. The hangover may be nothing more than a reaction to smoking, dancing, laughing, and shouting too much, plus staying up past bedtime.

This unglamorous view has little to recommend it except evidence. The overexertion theory explains why sometimes you can drink all night without penalty, while other times a single martini is suicidal. If you buy it, the key is to avoid drinking when you are tired, or to quit drinking before the party starts. The practicality of this advice may be somewhat limited.

Dehydration and indigestion. Alcohol puts the kidneys into high gear, draining fluids from the body. Along with the water goes an inordinate amount of magnesium. It's the magnesium depletion, or so some scientists believe, that is the main source of hangover jitters and tension headaches. Nausea and indigestion, on the other hand, are the result of damage to the linings of the stomach and intestines.

Probably the best way to deal with both syndromes is to limit the rate of absorption of alcohol. Quantity counts, but so does the speed with which you get loaded. Eating (preferably fat, bulky foods) helps; so will taking drinks in dilute form. The mixer of choice is water; carbonated brew gets through to the bloodstream faster. That's why champagne goes to the head so quickly.

After the evil deed is done, you are stuck. Coffee might help a bit—the caffeine counteracts tension headaches. Antacids, aspirin, and patience are recommended, but won't produce miracles.

Guilt and REM suppression. Next to the overexertion

theory, this depresses us most. One reason you may feel bad is that you think you ought to feel bad. Having a good time, especially with demon rum, just doesn't fit in with the Puritan tradition. It's no use protesting that *you* are above all that nonsense. Denial only strengthens the case.

Guilt may not be the sole culprit here. Alcohol, like many drugs, messes up ordinary sleep. Especially rapid eye movement (REM) sleep, which is believed to affect your mood the next morning. A couple of drinks suppress REM for a few hours, giving you just half the night to make up for lost time. This explains waking up sweating at three in the morning, or the particularly nasty dreams that follow two or three for the road. Really putting a bag on suppresses REM sleep completely, with the expected payoff the next morning. Dyed-in-the-wool alcoholics, incidentally, adjust and start REM-ing again.

Nothing helps the guilt or REM suppression hangover, except reform. Guilt may go a long way, though, in explaining why disgusting cures like raw eggs and Tabasco seem to work.

Congeners. Alcohol is not the only poison in booze. Virtually anything worth drinking—from daiquiris to Château d'Yquem—contains congeners, by-products of fermentation and distillation. Congeners were once believed to be the primary cause of hangovers. Alas, this is not the case; the little devils don't cause hangovers, they just make them worse.

To get the least hangover per ounce of alcohol, at the head of the list is cheap, highly filtered vodka. Flavorful Polish and Russian vodkas aren't as pure. Next best are distilled spirits that aren't aged—gin, inexpensive cordials. Aged whiskey is medium-high in congeners; red wine and brandy are the closest thing to Sterno.

HOW TO BUY AN ISLAND

Had enough of the runny-nosed brats next door who play touch football on your lawn at 6 A.M.? Fed up worrying about burglars and muggers and rapists setting up shop in your neighborhood? Well, it's not too late to do something about it—buy your own island.

With an estimated one million islands off the shores of North America, there are plenty to choose from. Of course, if you really want to live on your island, or at least be able to visit without investing a fortune in survival gear, the choice is narrowed considerably. A good island must be accessible, if not for guests, for grocery and fuel deliveries. It should have a fresh-water source, sufficient soil to maintain vegetation, reasonable drainage, and safe swimming conditions. Consider, too, that islands can take an awful pounding from the elements. A center ridge creating a lee shore, or a natural breakwater, offers some protection.

Best places to look today for a hospitable retreat include the Sea Islands (off the coast of Georgia), Long Island Sound, the Maine coast, and Puget Sound. Thousands of islands in the St. Lawrence and the Great Lakes are privately owned; here, the big virtues are accessibility and protected waters. Real-estate brokers generally maintain listings of available properties. To find an agent, check with the local chamber of commerce.

Should something domestic not suit your needs, have a look in the Caribbean, Mediterranean, or South Pacific. International brokers like J. T. Luyt (500 East Seventy-seventh Street, New York) and Previews, Inc. (49 East Fifty-third Street, New York), can shop for you just about anywhere. Remember, though, buying an island abroad can be very complicated. Foreigners may not legally own property in most of the world's unspoiled places. In practice, Americans do manage to own foreign islands through corporate covers. For the moment, property in Canada, most of the Caribbean, and Italy is available without resort to subterfuge. Turkey and Mexico are definitely closed.

Keep in mind, also, that buying an island doesn't mean it will be yours forever. The U.S. Marines are not likely to come to your rescue when the natives decide you are an imperialist running dog. Except, perhaps, if your cousin is Richard Helms.

HOW TO BUY AN ORIENTAL RUG

Once upon a time, when life was simple and Cadillacs had fins, Oriental rugs were something to cover floors with. Nicer than linoleum, but not as comfy as those $14.95-a-square-yard, two-inch-wool-pile, wall-to-wall jobs. Today every department store worthy of its escalator has a floor full of Orientals (or machine-made Belgian copies) and a wall display of silk prayer rugs too expensive to touch without gloves. Like as not, the whole enterprise is presided over by the smoothest middle-aged male salesperson in the store, the one who used to specialize in explaining why your sofa was eleven weeks overdue from the factory.

Since everyone has caught on, of course, there are no longer fabulous bargains to be had. The antique-rug prices are at least triple those of a decade ago, new-rug prices at least double. This does not mean Orientals aren't worth owning. How else is it possible to buy great original art for $1,000? And, for that matter, rugs may yet be a fair investment; antique Orientals appear to be on every rich Arab's shopping list.

The first rule for buying an Oriental rug is to choose one you like to look at. Being caught up in the snobbery of it all is fine, but the day will come when the last dinner-party guest has admired your good taste, and you still have to live with the thing. Beyond the obvious, knowing a few basics will go a long way to insuring reasonable value for your money.

Avoid auctions and on-the-spot purchases. The traveling rug auction is the hottest retailing gimmick around. With luck, you may save 10 percent off the best store price. More likely, you will end up overbidding. Auctions rarely give you a chance to examine the rugs carefully before sale. While out-and-out swindles can probably be rectified after the fact, it's not possible to return a rug because it shows worn spots in daylight or is beginning to dry-rot. The bidding itself will not give you much idea of the real value of a purchase, since friends of the house are usually in the audience to keep the proceedings lively.

Shopping in Middle Eastern bazaars is equally risky, unless you really know your rugs. Apart from the hazards of bargaining with experts, there is also the chance that shipping, insurance, and duty will turn a genuine find into an overpriced mistake. If you must buy abroad stick with merchants in the country of origin, where selection, if not price, may be exceptional.

Antiques shouldn't look that way. Handmade Orientals come in three categories—new, used, and antique. A new rug is just what it sounds like. Used rugs have been around, but not long enough to be classified as antiques. Their value is determined by their condition; a perfect used rug is worth as much as or more than a new rug of the same quality.

The turning point between used and antique is about World War I, though for purposes of paying import duties, the Feds define "antique" as 100 years old. Some unusual antique Orientals have scarcity value, like old coins or first editions. But generally, antiques are worth more because they are remarkably beautiful and durable. Nineteenth-century rugs are certain to have been made before the introduction of inferior synthetic dyes, which frequently speed the deterioration of the fiber strands. Visible minor repairs in a very old rug do not detract from its value; don't, however, purchase an antique less than 150 years old with threadbare spots or missing fringes. The likelihood you will be able to restore such a rug is remote. Antiques—both wool and silk—take on a quiet sheen from use which in no way reduces their quality.

When in doubt, count the knots. Orientals are constructed from rows of knots secured to a woven foundation. What you see are the loose ends of yarn sheared off to an even height. More knots means greater clarity and intensity in the design. It also means more work for the maker—a good weaver can tie only 1,000 knots an hour.

Though lots of things determine the value of a rug—age, condition, design, evenness of color, material, fashion—knot counting helps if you are comparing similar rugs. Block off a square inch on the back of the rug with a ruler, count the knots along two sides, and multiply. Middle Eastern wool rugs will have 150–700 knots per square inch, certain spectacular Indian rugs as many as 2,400. Chinese rugs of good quality are much less dense—expect only 50–150 per square inch.

The depth of pile, incidentally, is not a crucial factor in rug value. Middle Eastern Orientals average about a quarter inch; Chinese and shaggy, nomadic-variety Middle Eastern styles are a bit longer.

The more you look, the more you'll see. The first time out, chances are you will like what you are expected to like: geometrics dominated by dark blues and reds. There is nothing wrong with dark rugs—their popularity is a hold-over from the Victorians—and you may end up buying one. But check out the subtler varieties in cream, coral, pale blue, pink. Rich folks have bid up the price of the finest pastels—a large antique Oushak with knots of silk is hard to find at $200,000. Newer, less ambitious light-colored rugs don't cost any more than clichéd Sarouks or Bokharas, and may be nicer company over a lifetime.

HOW TO BUY A RACEHORSE

Have some spare cash burning a hole in your savings account? If you find the stock market too depressing and NFL football franchises too expensive, a thoroughbred may be just the ticket. The best way to buy one largely depends on your nerve and the dimensions of your wallet.

The auctions. A straightforward way to start is to bid

for a yearling colt or filly at auction. The two most prestigious auctions are held at Keeneland (Kentucky) in July and at Saratoga (New York) in August. Horses sold at these auctions are selected by the Keeneland Association and the Fasig-Tipton Company, and represent the cream of the

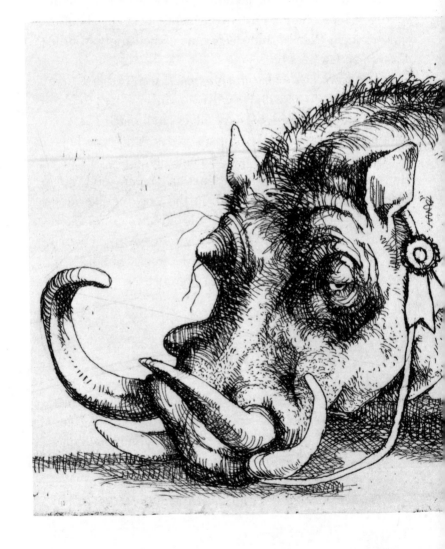

year's crop. (The *crème de la crème* usually is sold privately, if at all.) Cream isn't cheap. At Saratoga, for example, the minimum price is $5,000, and very few horses go for that little. How much more than that you'll pay depends on what the yearling looks like, what his blood-

lines are, and how much other people are willing to pay for him. A good-looking yearling with fashionable bloodlines will fetch $50,000 or more. The record price (as of this writing) is $715,000. For obvious reasons, you must prove you're credit-worthy before you'll be allowed into the auction ring. Instructions on doing so are given in the catalogues, available several weeks before the sales. It's also a good idea to have the help of an expert in the fine points of conformation and breeding: not everything with four legs and a tail is worth $53,637, the average price of yearlings sold at Keeneland in July 1975.

If you don't want to enter the big leagues at Keeneland or Saratoga, there are many other auctions held throughout the country, throughout the year. Some are for yearlings, some for horses of racing age (two years old and up), and some for breeding stock. The horses won't be as royally bred and the prices will be correspondingly lower. The Fasig-Tipton Company runs many of these, and a letter to them in Elmont, New York, will bring you a list of sales. Or you can check out the advertisements and lists of upcoming sales in either of two weekly magazines, *The Blood-Horse* and *The Thoroughbred Record*.

Once you own a yearling, it's a matter of waiting until he's officially two years old—a horse born anytime in the year is treated as if he were born January 1—and paying for upkeep and training. These will cost approximately $5,000 a year. Odds are slim you will find Prince Charming among the frogs, but a few unknowns have made it big.

Claiming sales. Tracks use claiming races to keep entries evenly matched. Any horse entered in a $15,000 claiming race, for example, is automatically for sale for

$15,000. To actually exercise a claim, you must already own a horse at the track, but it's a good bet that any horse risked in a claiming race is available privately at about the claim price, give or take a few thousand.

One advantage in claiming a horse over buying a yearling at auction is that you know, at least, that the horse is able to make it to the races and sometimes win. It is also possible to see the animal in action before handing over your cash. And you know approximately how much the beast is worth. (If Dobbin really is worth $75,000, do you think he'd be entered in a $15,000 claiming race?) There are, however, disadvantages. First, in the nature of things you won't be able to have the horse examined by a veterinarian before exercising a claim, and if something is wrong you're stuck. Second, you know that that bargain claimer isn't the next Kentucky Derby winner. The exception that proves the rule is Stymie, who earned $918,485 in his career, after having been claimed for $1,500. That was in 1943, and they're still talking about it.

Syndication. Thoroughbreds are often traded or sold privately. Extremely valuable horses—proven winners—are, however, frequently syndicated. Syndication technically means selling shares, typically thirty-two, in the stud fees (and sometimes the racing earnings) of the animal. In practice, big syndications have two purposes. First, the syndicator pays only capital-gains taxes on the sale price, rather than ordinary income tax on future profits. Second, the syndicator spreads risk. Most of the potential value of a horse like Secretariat is in stud fees, not prize money. People who purchase shares are really buying the right to use the horse at stud once each year for about ten years.

If the stud is a failure—that is, if his progeny prove to be glue-factory material—the investment may prove a bust.

Buying into a syndicate may prove quite difficult. Individual shares can be very expensive. A price of $50,000 is not unusual. Secretariat went for $190,000 a share, the record. (As this is written, efforts are being made to syndicate Wajima, which cost $600,000 as a yearling, for $200,000 a share.) And thoroughbred owners can be frightful snobs about their partners. They prefer old money—people whose ancestors stole their fortunes rather than those who have stolen their own. For a crack at one of the smaller, plebeian syndications ($20,000 to $30,000 per share) write for information to one of the bloodstock agencies. For openers try the Fasig-Tipton Company or the Cromwell Bloodstock Agency, Lexington, Kentucky.

What are the chances of making money in racehorses? Small, especially for the small investor. One study in the mid-sixties showed that the average racing thoroughbred cost 30 percent more to maintain than it earned, not even counting the initial capital investment. Very expensive horses do much better. A colt with impeccable bloodlines, priced in the $200,000 class, has a reasonable chance of earning back its price in prize money and syndication. Hence it takes a lot to make a lot. The real profits are for people who can afford to lose $100,000 a year in hopes of the occasional million.

C

HOW TO CALCULATE YOUR LIFE EXPECTANCY

No, we can't top Jeane Dixon. But if you are between twenty and sixty-five and reasonably healthy, this test provides a life-insurance-company's-eye view of the future.

(1) Start with 72.
(2) *Gender.*   If you are male, subtract 3.
                    If you are female, add 4.
                       [That's right, there's a seven-year spread between the sexes.]
(3) *Life Style.* (a) If you live in an urban area with a population over two million, subtract 2.
                       If you live in a town under ten thousand, or on a farm, add 2.
                       [City life means pollution, tension.]
              (b) If you work behind a desk, subtract 3.
                       If your work requires regular, heavy physical labor, add 3.
              (c) If you exercise strenuously (tennis, running, swimming, etc.) five times a week for at least a half hour, add 4. Two or three times a week, add 2.
              (d) If you live with a spouse or friend, add 5. If not, subtract 1 for every

ten years alone since age
twenty-five.

> [People together eat better,
> take care of each other,
> become less depressed.]

(4) *Psyche.*   (a) Sleep more than ten hours each night?
Subtract 4.

> [Excessive sleep is a sign of
> depression, circulatory diseases.]

(b) Are you intense, aggressive, easily
angered? Subtract 3.
Are you easygoing, relaxed, a
follower? Add 3.

(c) Are you happy? Add 1.
Unhappy? Subtract 2.

(d) Have you had a speeding ticket in the
last year? Subtract 1.

> [Accidents are the fourth-largest
> cause of death; first, in young
> adults.]

(5) *Success.*   (a) Earn over $50,000 a year? Subtract 2.

> [Wealth breeds high living,
> tension.]

(b) If you finished college, add 1.
If you have a graduate or
professional degree, add 2 more.

> [Education seems to lead to
> moderation; at least that's the
> theory.]

(c) If you are sixty-five or over and still

working, add 3. [Retirement kills.]

(6) *Heredity.* (a) If any grandparent lived to eighty-five, add 2.

If all four grandparents lived to eighty, add 6.

           (b) If either parent died of a stroke or heart attack before the age of fifty, subtract 4.

           (c) If any parent, brother, or sister under fifty has (or had) cancer or a heart condition, or has had diabetes since childhood subtract 3.

(7) *Health.* (a) Smoke more than two packs a day? Subtract 8.

One to two packs? Subtract 6.

One half to one? Subtract 3.

           (b) Drink the equivalent of a quarter bottle of liquor a day? Subtract 1.

           (c) Overweight by fifty pounds or more? Subtract 8. Thirty to fifty pounds? Subtract 4.

Ten to thirty pounds? Subtract 2.

           (d) Men over forty, if you have annual checkups, add 2.

Women, if you see a gynecologist once a year, add 2.

(8) *Age Adjustment.* Between thirty and forty? Add 2.

Between forty and fifty? Add 3.

Between fifty and seventy? Add 4.

Over seventy? Add 5.

It's no fun playing the game unless you know how well you've done. The table below tells what percentage of the population you will outlive, providing you make it to the specified age.

Age	60	65	70	75	80	85	90	95	100
Men	26%	36%	48%	61%	75%	87%	96%	99%	99.9%
Women	15%	20%	30%	39%	53%	70%	88%	97%	99.6%

HOW TO CAST YOUR BREAD UPON THE WATERS

A recent bus collision in Chicago resulted in complaints of injuries from twenty-seven riders. Trouble is, the police report that the bus had only seven passengers at the time of the accident.

HOW TO CHANGE YOUR NAME

Some names are losers. Research studies have shown (honest) that teachers give consistently lower grades to Percys and Ednas than to Peters and Lisas. And later on, when Percy applies for that lumberjack job, chances are he'll be shunned in favor of John or Michael—employers avoid applications with names that make them uncomfortable.

Should you have a reason, practical or aesthetic, for dropping your name, the simplest way is to just stop using it. Apply for a driver's license, register to vote, and pay your taxes with a new name. After some minor hassles the new name should stick. There is no law against calling yourself whatever you like, unless the idea is to fool creditors or elude the cops.

If you have qualms about changing overnight from Viola Bow to Nancy Smith without legal sanction, it's pretty easy to make the switch official in front of a judge. Though the details differ from state to state, a formal name change is rarely complicated enough to require a lawyer. Apply through the clerk's office of the local probate, surrogate, or superior court—a few phone calls should be enough to find the right place. After filing a set of forms you will be granted your day (more likely, your minute) in court.

Almost everyone who goes to the bother of the statutory procedure succeeds, though there are exceptions. In Massachusetts, a judge refused a request to adopt the name Cabot; the other Cabots, it seems, protested.

HOW TO CHARTER A YACHT

This winter, before you plunk down $105 a day for a plastic deck chair beside the pool of some plastic Hilton, consider what you are missing. For less money, you can charter a thirty-five-foot yacht, everything included, and explore the Caribbean.

Charters come in two styles: with crew, or bareboat.

"With crew" can mean high living all the way—private staterooms, maid service, lobster and champagne feasts. Be prepared to pay $75 to $300 a day per person for this kind of luxury.

Bareboating—renting a yacht the way you would rent a car from Avis—is much easier on the wallet. Comfortable boats for two, with no one to notice if you forget your bikini, average $50 to $100 a day. The catch, of course, is that you must have some sailing experience in order to go it alone. For ambitious novices, a few charter companies will compromise. They'll find a local sailor for hire to help with the hard parts, or just to stand by for emergencies. At least one bareboat charterer (Caribbean Sailing Yachts, Tortola, British Virgin Islands) will even teach you to sail on your own in a week or two.

Charters are possible just about anywhere in the Caribbean, though the most popular cruising is in the Virgin Islands. There waters are perfect for part-time sailors. Lots of tiny harbors to check out; no navigation problems since land is never more than ten miles away. More ambitious charters can be had farther south in the Windward and

Leeward islands. Here, islands are as much as fifty miles apart and passages between them are less sheltered.

The easiest way to rent a boat is through a broker. Big Caribbean brokers offer a choice of islands, yacht sizes, and luxury options. The most conveniently located agents are on the U.S. mainland. Try Stevens Yachts, Inc. (200 Park Avenue, New York), Peter Storm Charters (Smith Street, Norwalk, Connecticut), or World Yacht Enterprises (14 West Fifty-fifth Street, New York). They can give you specifics on bareboating proficiency requirements, reservations, and deposits. The U.S. Virgin Islands Tourist Office (in Chicago, New York, Miami, Washington) also keeps up-to-date lists of local charter companies. It's a good idea to think ahead on high-season charters. The brokers may be out of winter boats by September.

There is no need to stick to the Caribbean, though selection is more limited and prices are higher elsewhere. Charters in France and the western Mediterranean are nearly all fully crewed and primarily powerboats. World Yacht Enterprises represents 300 owners in the Mediterranean. One of their seventy-eight-foot yachts with a crew of four (sleeps six passengers) will set you back $4,000 a week in the summer season.

Chartering in Greece is considerably cheaper—that $4,000 French craft would be closer to $3,000 in the eastern Mediterranean. Hundreds of yachts based at Piraeus are ready to take you to the islands or up the Adriatic coast to Yugoslavia. Selecting a vessel unseen is fairly simple, since the Greek government rates commercial yachts. Category I craft, carrying four passengers in rather spartan conditions, fetch $100 or less a day; Category VIII's can be large diesel yachts with room for twelve passengers and as many crew. Contact Sparkman and Stephens, Inc. (11 East Forty-fourth Street, New York), John Trumpy and Sons (242 Royal Palm Way, Palm Beach, Florida), or Embassy Yachting (29 La Salle Street, Chicago). For the addresses of brokers in Greece write the Greek National Tourist Organization (601 Fifth Avenue, New York).

Of course, if you've just inherited a few hundred acres of downtown Houston or know General Thieu's Swiss bank account number, all this talk of economy yachts can be a bore. World Yacht Enterprises would be happy to lease something roomier. Perhaps the *Southern Breeze,* an ocean-fit pleasure boat registered in Panama. The ten-year-old yacht has five guest bedrooms, a dining room, and thirty-foot main salon, plus a crew of sixteen to keep things tidy. Should you become bored, the *Southern Breeze* offers scuba-diving and water-ski equipment, along with sophisticated communications equipment for stock-market watchers. A bargain, at $28,000 a week.

HOW TO CHECK THE ACCURACY OF A POSTAGE SCALE

Nine pennies weigh one ounce.

If you happen to be fresh out of pennies, try 1.06 silver dollars, 2.47 copper half-dollars, or two Hershey bars with almonds, unwrapped.

HOW TO CHOOSE A DOG

Within limits, dogs are what you make them. This doesn't mean, though, that good genes won't give you a head start. Dachshunds were specially bred to hunt badgers, Afghans to herd goats. Some less exotic possibilities:

Apartment dogs. Well, obviously, you must avoid large breeds that need more exercise than a Porsche 911—Great Danes, Irish Wolfhounds, Newfoundlands. A few big dogs, like St. Bernards, appear to adjust to sedentary lives, but are rarely as interesting or attractive as in outdoor settings. Among the dozens of small dogs, most have been selected for aggressiveness or territorial instinct. That's why they are so yappy with milk deliveries and vacuum cleaners. Fine, if you want a dog to signal the presence of the enemy. Unbearable, if the little savage insists on warning you about motorcycles two blocks away.

This still leaves a fair selection of small and medium-sized canines with appropriate dispositions. That singularly common pet, the Poodle, comes in three packages—Standard, Miniature, and Toy. All sizes tend to be intelligent and friendly; big Poodles, however, are quieter and more dignified. They are extremely easy to train, perfect city dogs if you don't mind owning a cliché.

If you are in love with small terriers (Yorkshires, Australians, Scotties), yet can't bear the racket, consider less frantic breeds. The Tibetan Lhasa Apso has lots of terrier-like characteristics—endless curiosity, a cheerful, unsuspicious demeanor—without classic terrier drawbacks. The Papillon, a foot-high toy breed with huge, erect ears and a silky coat, is unusually friendly for a 5–10 pound dog. One true terrier, the Dandie Dinmont, is notably more peaceful than its brethren.

Dogs for kids. The conventional wisdom, here, is to stick with larger dogs ready and able to tolerate abuse. Big dogs, especially females, tend to be more difficult to provoke. But practically any animal can be baited, and any animal that weighs 150 pounds—say, a Newfoundland or St. Bernard—becomes dangerous when angry. Toys and small terriers, on the other hand, are pretty harmless no matter how mad they get. All the risk, in this case, rests on the dog.

The solution lies in compromise—choosing among larger, untemperamental terriers and peaceful hunting dogs. Prime candidates include the Golden Retriever, Beagle, Cocker Spaniel, Poodle, Bouvier des Flandres, Collie, Bull Terrier, and Old English Sheepdog. The Bull Terrier, incidentally, is the ultimate pacifist. One owner reports that his champion Bull Terrier, after being harassed by an angry Pekingese, simply picked the smaller animal up by the neck and dumped it in a wastebasket.

Guard dogs. The overwhelming majority of guard dogs are German Shepherds, due largely to long popular experience with the breed and their reputation for dependability. Doberman Pinschers are considered more dangerous and difficult to control, though there's no particular evidence this is true. Their notoriety probably stems from the vicious Dobermans bred for sentry work in Germany during World War I. In fact, any dog trained for attack is a liability when it's not on duty. No one has perfected a breed that is dependable in every circumstance.

Far better, then, to use a dog's natural guard instinct solely for warning and deterrence. Boxers are easily trained as guards and sufficiently formidable in appearance to scare muggers and burglars. The Bull Mastiff, Standard Schnauzer, and Rhodesian Ridgeback have much the same advantages. One other possibility, where it's the bluff that counts: the Bulldog. While English Bulldogs are immensely strong, they are absolute pussycats with people.

HOW TO CHOOSE A FEDERAL PRISON

Sure, we know it was your accountant's fault. But these days some of the best people are doing time. If you are planning to stash a key on your next trip home from Mexico, or even just donate your grocery lists to the National Archives, the following should be indispensable.

> ❁ Good in its class
> ❁ ❁ Merits a detour
> ❁ ❁ ❁ Worth the trip

❁ ❁ *Allenwood*. Located in central Pennsylvania, a few hours' drive from the offices of most of America's expensive lawyers. Allenwood is what the Feds call a "short term" prison, meaning there are no bars on the windows and the guards don't carry .38's. Sports facilities include indoor and outdoor tennis courts (Jeb Stuart Magruder was the visiting pro) and a weight room. Horseback riding can be arranged on request, though you may have to pitch in and herd cattle. The food is a decided drawback, but improves on

weekends when visitors share the cafeteria. Some guests also complain about the breakfast hours (6:00 to 6:15).

Apart from watching the scenery—nice view of the Allegheny Mountains from the terrace—and collecting autographs (recent departures include Clifford Irving, Bobby Baker, Egil Krogh, Carmine De Sapio), things can get pretty tedious at Allenwood. A pity the federal government doesn't need any license plates.

✿ *Danbury*. The Connecticut prison for those who make mistakes too large for Allenwood. Danbury was "undiscovered" until the authorities had the clever idea of inviting the Berrigan draft-resister set. In our view, the place has been oversold, though we do approve of the well-kept grounds.

Lewisburg. While some favor the Big House look, it's not our cup of tea. If you want to go to prison in Pennsylvania, stick with Allenwood. Lewisburg is much too large (1,500 inmates) to provide individual attention or a sense of intimacy with the architecture. It has had its share of notables—Jimmy Hoffa, Morton Sobell—but generally the crowd is a bit rough at the edges. About half the guys are dope pushers or robbers. The food makes Howard Johnson's look good.

✿ ✿ ✿ *Lompoc*. The jewel in the Bureau of Prisons chain, Lompoc's campus is located about a hundred miles from San Clemente. Its modern buildings err on the cold side. But this is more than made up by the nine-hole golf course and driving range, tennis court, handball court, and jogging track. Guards wear gray double-knit slacks and blue blazers; cheery, yet so practical for the Southern California climate. The dorm rooms offer little privacy. V.I.P. guests may be able to arrange accommodations, though, in one of the intimate doubles.

Marion. America's model maximum-security prison. That is to say, the worst thing that has happened to incarceration since Alcatraz. The average inmate at Marion is up for twenty years. We can't believe anyone will make it that long on the 77-cents-a-day food budget (1971 figures— they must spend more now, what with the price of Wonder bread and beans). Summers in southern Illinois can be rather too warm. Entertainment centers on behavior therapy, a polite way of making life so unpleasant that you turn straight.

HOW TO CHOOSE A GERMAN WINE

German white wines are fantastic bargains. While three or four dollars nets you only an adequate, assembly-line, lowest-common-denominator wine from California or France, for the same amount it is possible to purchase a truly great German bottle.

Naturally, there's a catch. Assembly-line California wines can be purchased with mere cash, but it practically takes a Ph.D. to figure out exactly what you are getting in German wines. And not surprisingly, cost is not a reliable measure of value. All the confusion about labels makes it easy for the big shippers to push Volkswagen-quality bottles at Mercedes-style prices.

Knowing a few rules, though, can get you a long way, far enough to separate the rip-offs from the good buys.

First, some fairly painless history. The small German wine industry is fragmented into tens of thousands of individually owned plots producing under a couple of thousand labels. Until 1971, the only remotely serious, government-sanctioned effort to protect the public from chaos was to label the small group of "natural" wines, those wines fermented without adding extra sugar. This is a more useful device for classifying wine than it might sound, since grapes with sufficient natural sugar all produce pretty good wine. Trouble is, it discriminated against many wines that were also quite good, and inspired a lot of white-collar crime. Even the most respectable vintners cheated now and then, adding a touch of grape sugar to make up for a sunless summer.

Enter a new set of government regulations, designed in theory to satisfy both the capitalists and the consumers. The language of labeling was cleaned up, defining precisely the quality characteristics of German wine which theretofore had been largely advertising copy. To make buying easier, 90 percent of the place names were legally banished, their wines consolidated into a master list. In return, sellers also got some breaks. A middle category of wines was established, permitting producers to add sugar to high-quality wines which fall short of the deluxe category. Less sensibly, a bunch of fourth-rate wines bearing made-up names were slipped into the new middle category, rather than being demoted to oblivion.

Here's how to pick 'em under the new law:

—The wines in slender green bottles are from the Moselle Valley; those in brown, from the Rhine. While there is immense variation in each group, Moselles tend to be fruitier and sharper, Rhine's more delicate and perfumy.

—The three new quality categories, from the top, are Qualitätswein mit Prädikat (QmP), Qualitätswein bestimmter Anbaugebiete (QbA), and Tafelwein. Forget the Tafelwein; little or none is exported anyway. QmP wines will generally be sweeter and subtler than QbA's, but the big bargains will be among the QbA's.

—Never got suckered into a wine called Liebfraumilch, Schwarze Katze, or Moselblümchen. Also avoid, where possible, wines sold simply by brand name, like Blue Nun or Hanns Christof. They are not bad, just overpriced.

—QbA and QmP wine labels show the township and vineyard of origin: a Wehlener Sonnenuhr comes from the Sonnenuhr vineyard in the township of Wehlen. Not all Wehlen wines (or, for that matter, Wehlener Sonnenuhr wines) taste exactly alike, but there is enough similarity to form a general impression. QbA's are apt to vary more within a vineyard since the consolidation of names has melded together so many individual plots. The clearest guarantee of uniformity is estate bottling—in German, Erzeuger-Abfüllung.

—QmP wines can carry extra designations of quality associated with natural sweetness. The ones you'll see are Spätlese and Auslese. Both are too sweet to drink with a main course. Try one with dessert, or instead of dessert.

—Vintage years mean a lot in German wines because of the fickle weather. Good wine districts all occasionally suffer cloudy summers and early frosts. The shorter the season, the lighter the wine, with far fewer vineyards managing enough natural sugar to meet the QmP requirements. Lesser vintages are not only less sweet—a dubious quality on its own—but less flavorful as well. Spätlese and Auslese wines last eight years or more in the bottle without serious deterioration; other German whites are best drunk within four years of the harvest. Note, too, that bottle age changes German wines, and not necessarily for the worse. They tend to lose their fresh grapy tang, but gain a subtler, more complex taste and smell.

—Rating the recent vintages: 1974, B; 1973, C; 1972, B; 1971, A; 1970, B; 1969, B. The 1971 is very special. Many believe it is the proverbial "wine of the century." What's left of the vintage is pretty expensive, though. The special bargains should be in the 1970's and 1972's.

HOW TO CLIMB MOUNT SINAI

By camel, naturally—need you ask?

Kissinger and Sadat permitting, three-day trips to Suez and Mount Sinai can be arranged through the Israeli tourist bureaus Egged Tours and United Tours of Tel Aviv. Travel is by bus or by plane—Arquia flies to Sharm-el-Sheik or to a small airfield near St. Katarina.

Stop overnight at St. Katarina, an ancient monastery founded in 530 by the emperor Justinian, now occupied by a few Orthodox Christian monks and a score of brown-robed Bedouin tribespeople. Accommodations rate high on authenticity: cloistered dormitory, narrow cots, and prayer bells tolling at all hours. Wake-up call is at 4 A.M., when, by starlight, a teen-age Bedouin will help you onto your camel and lead you up the Holy Mountain. By sunrise you will have reached the summit, with its view of the Biblical birthplace of the world.

HOW TO CONFOUND YOUR ENEMIES

Be inspired by the example of defeated Presidential candidate Hubert Humphrey, who was unreliably reported to have responded to the election-night news with "Whoopee, we lost!"

HOW TO CONSTRUCT A SAFE TRICYCLE

The Bureau of Public Safety, a part of the Food and Drug Administration, commissioned a $21,000 study on how to reduce tricycle accidents. Conclusion: add a fourth wheel.

HOW TO CURE INSOMNIA

If you have trouble sleeping, join the crowd. Every night some twenty million insomniacs take pills, choke down Ovaltine, don masks, or watch Johnny Carson's monologue, mostly in vain. These desperate souls have made sleep a recession-proof growth industry, with assorted exotica like "white noise" sources and biofeedback machines leading the way. The biggest benefactor of this devotion to unconsciousness is, of course, the corner drugstore. Compared to the army of barbiturate freaks, heroin addicts are an endangered species.

Since no one really knows what sleep is or why it is necessary, remedies for insomnia are pretty much all seat-of-the-pants. Take your choice:

Pills. Dozens of chemicals, swallowed or injected in sufficient quantity, will knock you out for eight hours. None of them, unfortunately, is likely to also provide a decent night's rest. Barbiturates (Nembutal, Seconal, Luminal), the most widely prescribed hypnotics, are typical. The first few times, they put you to sleep, but leave you a touch groggy the next morning. Tolerance develops rapidly—larger and larger doses are needed to achieve the same effect—until really massive amounts become necessary. After a month or two of steady use, all barbiturates can do is generate a few hours of unsatisfying sleep and a wicked hangover. Addiction is a common, if not inevitable, bonus.

Other hypnotics vary in specifics, but share many of the awful features of barbiturates. Chloral hydrate interferes less with normal sleep patterns and won't kill when mixed with alcohol, but may cause ulcers and liver damage. Doriden, Placidyl, Noludar, and methaqualone (Quaalude) can all generate addiction and mess up the crucial, deep stage of normal sleep. Over-the-counter sedatives like Nytol and Sominex are not very dangerous, but they don't work well either. Nonprescription sleeping pills usually contain methapyrilene and scopolamine. Too little to put you out, enough to cause occasional dizziness and memory loss.

Probably the best of a bad lot are tranquilizers called benzodiazepines (Valium, Librium, Dalmane). Taken in small doses, they reduce insomnia-causing anxiety without doing massive damage to the sleep cycle. And while it may be possible to become addicted to them, tolerance buildup is very slow. Side effects are rare, but not unheard of.

Home remedies. The great advantages of alcohol as a sedative are that it's cheap, available, and tasty. The disadvantages are that it's dangerous, addicting, and ineffective. Used infrequently, the nightcap is harmless enough. But over the long haul, alcohol-induced sleep is just like pill-induced sleep.

Surprisingly, there is evidence that the other classic home remedy, warm milk, really does work. Milk and, for that matter, most protein-rich foods contain tryptophane, the closest thing yet to nature's own sleep potion. Large doses

have, at the very least, a mild sedative effect and actually encourage the kind of sleep thought to be most refreshing. Along with tryptophane, a score of amino acids are thought to induce sleep. No one is prepared to prescribe amino acids for insomnia—when barbiturates were introduced, they were hailed as the perfect drugs. You are welcome to dose yourself, however, with a bedtime snack.

Stimulus control. Fear of insomnia is self-fulfilling. The more worried you become about getting to sleep, the less chance you have for success. In fact, bedtime worrying of any sort is likely to cause chronic insomnia, or so the theory goes. Once you associate bed with anxiety, the insomnia will persist after the real source of worry has passed.

Now, advising people to stop worrying is about as useful as telling people to stop breathing. But it is possible to break the association of worry with sleep. The first rule is: never lie awake for more than thirty minutes. If you can't sleep, don't try. Get up and read something, or watch an old Pat O'Brien movie on the tube. No matter how long it takes to get to sleep this way, don't reset the alarm. A few three-hour nights won't hurt.

Sleep therapists believe that anybody in reasonable health will get enough sleep following this system. Insomniacs who claim to sleep just a few hours a night are (a) exaggerating, (b) dreaming they are awake while asleep, or (c) among the select few that need little or no sack time.

Sleep clinics. If warm milk and calm thought don't work, the sleep clinic is a last resort. Sleep clinics have been around for quite a while, but only recently were discovered by journalists. The clinics wire you up, observe your sleep performance for a few nights, and then try to prescribe a regimen to get you back to normal patterns.

Usually the solution is straightforward, since most insomniacs who make it to a clinic are not suffering from neurological diseases. EEG recordings can provide proof of drug-ruined sleep, or prove to a skeptic that he or she actually does get enough rest. The most conservative treatment for diehards is psychotherapy to find out what really is wrong.

Less ambitious approaches include hypnosis and biofeedback training. Hypnosis is much older, but the concept behind biofeedback is much the same. The key is to learn to relax. Under hypnosis, posthypnotic suggestion cues the subject to think clean thoughts as head meets pillow. With biofeedback devices, patients are taught to recognize, and then imitate, the tranquil, half-awake stage that occurs naturally before sleep. The special attraction of biofeedback is the ease with which people learn the technique—transcendental meditation without the guru.

Even if you beat insomnia, your problems may not be over. (See "How to Cure Snoring.")

HOW TO CURE SNORING

If you snore, or—more to the point—if you sleep with someone who does, you know that snoring is no joke. It has destroyed marriages, created bloody feuds in hotels and railroad compartments, and tormented millions with guilt and mental anguish. Stanford University researchers have even tied snoring to a disease called Sleep Apnea Syndrome, which can lead to high blood pressure. Hardly anyone is immune: one out of every five persons has a snoring problem. The affliction can beset you at any age, and women are as likely to snore as men.

Snoring is no respecter of status. Winston Churchill was a famous snorer. He was auditioned at 55 decibels—about as loud as a doorbell. Mussolini snored, according to the memoirs of various ladies who knew him, and so did a long list of U.S. Presidents, including Washington, both Adamses, Pierce, and FDR. Teddy Roosevelt snored, once so loudly in a hospital that complaints were filed by almost every patient in the ward.

What is snoring? Time out for a little heavy anatomy. The source of the problem is the soft palate and the posterior faucial area. The fauces is the critical region—that's the space bounded by the soft palate, the base of the tongue, and the palatine arches. As humans age, the palate muscles tend to loosen up, resonating as air passes by. Therefore snoring is more common in older people, but some children snore. So do elephants, camels, cows, sheep, cats, dogs, chimps, gorillas, zebras, and buffalo.

If the cause is structural, surgery may be the cure. Doctors occasionally recommend removal of enlarged tonsils and adenoids, surgery to correct deviated septums (few of us have perfect nasal septums), removal of nasal polyps, and, in rare instances, removal of the uvula, which hangs like a grape from the soft palate above the base of the tongue.

The scalpel may seem a radical way out, but once it is done, it is done. Nonsurgical methods for curing snoring require more time and much self-control. But even here, a complete cure is possible in about 50 percent of all cases. Only 20 percent are hopeless incurables.

For some, snoring is caused by allergies, especially allergies to air pollution and cigarette smoke. Hence antihistamines and decongestants may help temporarily. Allergists are partial to endless rounds of desensitization injections. This cure, however, is worse than the disease.

Some of the most effective anti-snoring methods require ridiculous amounts of self-discipline. If you smoke, give it up. Smoking irritates the pharyngeal area, and that, needless to say, is very, very bad. Don't overindulge: excessive eating, especially before bedtime, may create a postnasal drip, while alcohol does unpleasant things to the aforementioned pharyngeal tissues. Don't overexert, either. And avoid peanuts and fried foods. There is evidence—believe it or not—that a low-fat, low-salt diet also helps.

Before attempting something dramatic, try the simple solution of changing position in bed. Most experts agree that sleeping on one's back with an open mouth generates first-class snoring. Better to sleep on one side, or on your stomach. If you must sleep on your back, wedge a small pillow under your chin. Perhaps you'll need to keep it in place with elastic bands, at least until you develop the habit of extending your neck and keeping your mouth shut during sleep.

Keeping your mouth shut is a big part of the cure, but if you can't do it alone, don't give up. For decades the Patent Office has been cluttered with devices designed to help. Mouth restrainers force the sleeper to breathe through the nose. A common one is a plastic plug that fits between the teeth and lips, then is secured to the victim's head with elastic bands.

Chin restrainers work pretty much the same way, making it impossible for the wearer to sleep with his or her mouth open. The most famous is the Thomas collar, sold by Trubuck, Inc., of Elkhart, Indiana, and used chiefly by orthopedists in treating neck injuries. It's hard to believe, though, that anyone has ever gotten a decent night's sleep in one of these things.

D. Horwich, a widely quoted anti-snoring authority, takes the position that snore-prevention devices only coddle the snorer and prevent coming to grips with the real problem. Horwich rejects physical crutches and stands behind positive thinking. He suggests self-hypnosis, or autosuggestion, by which the snorer repeats over and over: "I will not snore tonight or any other night," until the subconscious turns belly up and cooperates. Good luck.

Some snorers find relief in a regimen of phonetic exercises to tense and tighten the muscles of the soft palate through murmuring "ahhhhh." Two famous routines, called the Flack Exercises after their inventor, aim to train the muscles that keep the mouth shut. Very simply, Flack suggests holding something between the teeth for ten minutes each night before bed. This builds up jaw muscles; start modestly and increase gradually, or you will find yourself with a charley horse in an unusual location.

The second Flack Exercise strengthens and shortens the muscles which hold the lower jaw and tongue forward. To begin, press your fingers firmly on the front of the chin while pushing forward with your jaw muscles. Go easy on this one, too. It will take only two minutes or so before your muscles begin to protest.

For stubborn snorers, other first-aid measures include sleeping on a wooden pillow like the Japanese, who are alleged never to snore. American Indians don't snore either (or stutter), probably because Indian children are taught to sleep with closed mouths to prevent throat diseases. One woman stopped snoring forever when she stopped wearing curlers to bed. You may find relief if you wear a nightcap; or better yet, drink one. The Vermont doctor, predictably, suggests honey and cider vinegar.

HOW TO CURE TENNIS ELBOW

For those among you who have never been cursed by the tennis god, murmur a prayer, knock on wood (or aluminum), and skip this entry. You cannot possibly know the special hell reserved for martyrs of the courts.

The human body, particularly the arm, was not designed to play tennis. Perhaps in a few hundred thousand years—assuming good tennis players breed faster than bad ones—the species will adjust to the unusual demands of the game. But for the moment, we are stuck. Tennis elbow is an inflammation of the epicondyle, the knobby end of the upper arm bone. Each time you hit a ball with your arm bent, the shock is borne by your forearm muscle, and ultimately by the tendon that connects the forearm muscle to the epicondyle. The weakest link in the chain is the last link; after a few hundred or a few thousand off-balance whacks at the ball, your epicondyle gives up. Not only can you no longer swing a racket; any activity which requires forearm power—shaking hands, carrying a suitcase—becomes exquisitely painful.

The treatment for tennis elbow depends upon how badly you've mangled the epicondyle. Usually a six-week vacation from tennis will be sufficient. In more serious cases, injections of anti-inflammation drugs like cortisone are needed to hasten healing. For an unlucky few, surgery is required to clear out chips of shattered epicondyle and reconnect the tendon to the upper arm bone.

Neither rest nor surgery, however, will reduce the chances of doing it again, once you get back on the court. The only long-term cure involves strengthening the forearm muscles and learning to play tennis properly.

The muscle part is comparatively easy. Since the forearm controls movement of the wrist, the best exercise is to move your clenched fist up and down at the wrist, with your arm extended straight in front. First on its own, then under tension provided by pushing down on the fist with your other hand.

Tennis lessons may also help, because the root of the problem is bad form. A perfect tennis player could never contract tennis elbow because he or she would never stroke the ball with a bent arm. With the elbow locked, the shock of the ball passes harmlessly through the epicondyle and is dissipated in the big muscles of the upper arm and shoulder. Since no player has perfect form—even Ken Rosewall bends his elbow occasionally on an awkward shot—everyone risks damage to the epicondyle. Still, the more classic your form, the less you tempt fate. Professional tennis players are almost immune.

HOW TO DECLARE BANKRUPTCY

DUntil recently, bankruptcy was the exclusive province of the very rich. The rest of us just didn't have the good sense to tell the collection agencies and credit-card companies where to go when the going got rough. In fact, the right to start afresh, without debt, is so fundamental that it's mentioned in the first article of the Constitution.

What bankruptcy really means. If your debts are greater than your assets, and you don't want to spend the rest of your days bailing out, personal bankruptcy may be the answer. The mechanics are simple enough. You petition a special federal court for bankruptcy, listing all your property and the amount owed to each creditor. The court orders the creditors to lay off, auctions the property to make partial restitution, and sends you on your way. Creditors have no further claims—if they try to dun you, they are risking contempt of court and civil suit. Should you care to compensate an old creditor, post-bankruptcy, it is still your option.

Exemptions. Bankruptcy can be even better than it sounds. Depending on your state, certain personal property is placed beyond the reach of bill collectors, no matter how much you owe. The biggest loophole is equity in a house or farm, but clothing, furniture, tools, books, life insurance, a small savings account, and an automobile may also be exempted. If your state is tougher than most—Iowa permits an $800 house exemption; North Dakota, a whopping $40,000—it may actually pay to change residence. For purposes of bankruptcy, you need reside in a state for only three months and a day.

Two other points to remember:

—A house or farm is protected only if you have the foresight to legally declare it to be a "homestead" prior to petitioning for bankruptcy. Homesteading merely requires a formal notarized declaration at a county clerk's office; it costs only a few dollars to register the declaration, and the form takes just a half hour or so to complete.

—Mortgaged property is never protected. Unless you can keep up the payments on the car or house or mink coat, they can be legally repossessed.

The catch. Not all kinds of debts can be discharged through bankruptcy. If it cares to, the IRS can hound you to your grave. So can state and local tax authorities. Bankruptcy has no effect on child support, alimony, or obligations incurred while defrauding someone. For that matter, if you burn down your neighbors' house or steal their life savings, they can still sue to collect, after bankruptcy. Federal law also prohibits the use of bankruptcy more than once every six years.

Chapter 13, the Wage-Earner Plan. If you can't face the shame of bankruptcy, or are afraid it will ruin your career, there is still a way to hold your creditors at bay. All you have to do is petition the bankruptcy court to set up a Wage-Earner Plan, a formal agreement between you and the court to pay off your debts over a three-year period. As long as you keep to the payment schedule, creditors are powerless to attach your property or garnish your wages. And if you find you can't meet the schedule—80 percent give up—you still have the option of declaring bankruptcy.

Private debt consolidators will often perform the same service, either refinancing your debts or getting creditors to agree to wait. But Chapter 13 is generally cheaper. The court-appointed trustee's fee is just 10 percent of the debt.

The big disadvantage of a Wage-Earner Plan is that you must eventually cough up all the money owed. In exchange, you save face. How it will influence your credit rating is less clear. It's true that a Chapter 13 plan shows you care, but it also signals any would-be creditors that you are a prime candidate for ordinary bankruptcy. By contrast, once you have declared personal bankruptcy, business associates will know that you can't do it again for a long time.

When you need a lawyer. In nine cases out of ten a lawyer can do you no good here, or so some legal experts maintain. A lawyer will charge $500 to $1,500 to file the necessary forms and appear at your bankruptcy hearing. Generally, the court will offer the necessary help on paper work, anyway, and a lawyer will provide little more than moral support.

Lawyers are necessary, however, if your bankruptcy is likely to be challenged by creditors, or if you are too shy to demand your rights. The lawyer, incidentally, may cost you nothing. The fee will be paid from the proceeds of the auction, since, as you might expect, bankruptcy legal bills have priority over other debts.

HOW TO DO WELL BY DOING GOOD

In the early days of television, the networks lobbied vigorously (and successfully) for the Federal Communications Commission to set aside one channel in each viewing area for educational TV. The result: no airspace for a fourth network, and no extra competition for a slice of the advertising billions.

HOW TO EARN EXTRA CASH AT HOME IN YOUR SPARE TIME

Ever wondered what to do with those old mason jars in the basement?

The Sigma Chemical Company of St. Louis needs (live) fireflies. The going rate is $3.00 per thousand, but bonuses are offered to volume collectors.

Before you head for the backyard, it might be wise to write Sigma (Box 14508, St. Louis, Missouri 63178) for shipping instructions.

HOW TO EAT CHEAP BUT GOOD IN PARIS

You don't have to be rich to enjoy Paris, but it helps. Here, the good life is practiced as an art form, with temptations in every quarter. A seventeenth-century town house on the Ile St. Louis with a view of the Seine and Notre Dame? Only $2,000 a month. Lunch at Taillevent, duck with lemon and a good Burgundy? About $50. Perhaps a leather brief-case from Hermès on the rue St. Honoré? Just $600.

It's still possible, though, to dine well in the City of Light for less than the price of Swiss steak at a Ramada Inn. The

French—or at least some of the French—care enough about real food to support the best neighborhood restaurants in the world. Providing your tastes don't run to *foie gras* and lobster, any of the following should satisfy.

Vagenende (142 boulevard St. Germain). On first glance, it's hard to believe this restaurant could be inexpensive. The interior is pure Belle Epoque—mirrored walls, Tiffany glass, brass ornaments, dark polished wood. In fact, the Vagenende caters to students from the nearby Sorbonne, local shopkeepers, and tourists on a budget. No surprises on the complete dinners: simple hors d'oeuvres, grilled meats and stews, nice fruit tarts, adequate cheese selection. Beaujolais by the pitcher, and friendly, if harried, service.

La Petite Chaise (36 rue de Grenelle). Most Parisian restaurants with bargain dinners tantalize their patrons with à la carte specialties at three times the price. Not so this establishment in the heart of the staid 7th arrondissement. The menu at $5.00 (including wine) gives you a choice of twenty appetizers and eighteen main courses. The *pissaladière*, a tart filled with anchovy, olive, and onion, makes an excellent beginning; try the *cotelette Pojarsky* afterward. Then, for dessert, sample Chef Largeaud's fresh fruit salad or pastry.

La Cigale (7 rue de la Roquette). La Cigale is located in an unfashionable part of Paris, a place where people work hard for a living. If you risk a visit (it's near the Place de la Bastille) you'll be rewarded with a generous country-style meal for under $5.00, including tip: liver terrine, *quenelle de brochet* or beef stew, pastry or cheeses.

55

Au Beaujolais (17 rue de Lourmel). One of several restaurants of the same name in Paris, this one is a cheerful, noisy bistro specializing in Burgundian cuisine. The super-garlicky Lyonnaise sausage served with boiled potato is fabulous. We also like the roast chicken with cheese sauce and the hot apple tart. If you are adventurous, try the Ferchuse. We won't describe it. Warning: it takes discipline to stay under $5.00.

Alice (198 boulevard Malesherbes). A new restaurant with clever ideas and incredibly low prices. The $5.00 menu features hors d'oeuvres, steak with a bordelaise sauce, and pastry. Or, for $3.00, make a meal from the hors d'oeuvres cart, with a dozen cold meats, fish, and vegetables. Country wine by the pitcher is just $1.50.

La Bonne Table (5 rue de Séveste). Ideal for restoring the spirits after a morning trudging around Montmartre. The standard $4.00 meal includes a choice of ten appetizers, a cold meat platter with vegetables, and a fattening dessert. The quality of the food and welcome outweigh the rather shabby appearance.

Chez Ginette (101 rue Caulaincourt-Paris). France's colonial adventures in North Africa paid few dividends. Couscous—steamed grains with meat—is one of them. Chez Ginette is a good place to try couscous. Wash it down with the proprietor's good Algerian wine. Forget dessert.

Relais Villette (25 rue Corentin-Cariou). Consider the $4.00 menu, one of the great bargains in Paris: mussels or *salade niçoise*, roast beef, cheese, desserts. The catches: (a) the Relais Villette is as far from the center of Paris as is possible without leaving the city; (b) the restaurant serves only at lunch.

Au Boeuf Gros Sel (70 rue de Volga). Another fine ɔld bistro, far from the high-rent district. The $5.00 menu includes a cold beef salad or herring in mustard sauce to begin, then *pot-au-feu*, then cheeses, then pastries. A good Beaujolais to go with this feast will add $4.00 to the check.

Luu Dinh (6 rue Thouin). One of the first Vietnamese restaurants in Paris. Luu Dinh remains very cheap and very good, in spite of the crowds of students who invade it every night. Remember the shrimp with ginger and the pork Peking style.

HOW TO END THE HEROIN EPIDEMIC

Look on the bright side. Unlike most great problems of the day—nuclear proliferation, the arms race, Third World poverty, street crime—the solution to the heroin crisis is staring us in the face. The possibilities:

Enforce the drug laws. The obvious remedy. So obvious, in fact, that everybody with a stake in the solution has agreed to ignore its one minor flaw—enforcement can't work. After half a century, billions of tax dollars invested, hysterical federal and state legislation, international treaties, police-state customs checks, and bribes to opium farmers, there are more addicts than ever before. How many more, we really don't know. Figures as high as a half million have been bandied about by the Bureau of Narcotics and Dangerous Drugs around appropriations time. A congressional committee guessed that 250,000 Americans had steady habits in 1971. Taking the 250,000 figure and the committee's conservative estimate that each victim spends about $20 a day on maintenance, addicts must raise on the order of $1.8 billion each year. Perhaps three fourths of that is double-counted—addicts retail heroin to each other at astronomical markups to finance their own habits—so the total cash needed to keep everyone going is something like $500 million—$500 million that must be earned or begged or stolen.

The reasons law enforcement hasn't (and couldn't) work are plain. As a practical matter, stiff penalties for dealing have little effect because judges and juries are rarely willing to impose them. When courts do get tough, the street price of dope goes up, increasing the financial incentives of sellers, and raising the ante for crooked cops. Don't forget, too, that each time heroin prices increase, burglaries and robberies by addicts must also increase.

The Nixonian War on Drugs concentrated on stopping heroin at the border. This didn't work either. Something like 5 percent of imports were captured. We are probably lucky more wasn't seized. Every pound caught by customs means that much more crime to pay for the dope that does make it. Some experts argue that the War on Drugs had the additional effect of enforcing organized crime's monopoly on drug importation, driving the street price yet higher.

Should the customs fuzz ever figure out how to cut the drug traffic significantly, dealers will have a surprise for them. Narcotic concentrates one thousand times as powerful as heroin—a few hundred pounds would supply the yearly needs of North America—can be manufactured with currently available technology.

Cure the addicts. If we can't take drugs away from the addict, how about taking the addict away from drugs? That's the idea behind the Public Health Service hospital at Lexington, Kentucky, therapy communes like Daytop and Synanon, and hundreds of state and local rehabilitation programs. Unfortunately, heroin addiction isn't very curable. It is easy to detoxify addicts, very easy if drugs are used to facilitate gradual withdrawal. But the addiction remains. For reasons much theorized about, though not understood, most detoxified addicts—more than 90 percent —return to heroin. The enormous New York and California rehab efforts have generated miserable results. In the first seven years of its existence, the California program treated eight thousand people, yet could claim to have discharged only a few hundred true abstainers.

Therapy communities, which rely on group pressure and shelter from day-to-day problems to ease addicts back to society, have proved to be equally expensive failures. For every ex-addict served, dozens have slipped back to drugs. Synanon acknowledges the problem quite candidly. They expect ex-addicts to remain within the Synanon community for life. All this is particularly astonishing, since the therapy communities accept only highly motivated volunteers.

Fight addiction with drugs. Heroin is lots of fun. That, presumably, is why addicts inject enough of the stuff to become addicted in the first place. If you took away the thrill, addicts might quit on their own.

They might, but they don't. Several non-addicting antagonists to heroin have, in fact, been developed which eliminate the high from shooting dope. An experiment with one such chemical, Cyclazocine, reveals the logical fallacy behind attacking addiction with non-addicting drugs. From a group of 186 addicts, only 33 were willing to spoil their future highs by taking the blocking drug. Of the 33 only 11 stayed off heroin for two years. This is a much better success rate than non-drug treatment has ever achieved, yet it's still pretty dismal. Cyclazocine removes any temporary temptation to go back to junk, but has no impact on the long-term suffering experienced by addicts—the years of anxiety and depression that only narcotics seem to relieve. After struggling for a few months, addicts typically drop the Cyclazocine.

Switch addiction. A standard technique for detoxifying addicts is to substitute other narcotics for heroin, and then gradually decrease the dose. This gradual approach reduces the physical discomfort of withdrawal. As important, it eases the emotional impact. Morphine (or even heroin) can be used for withdrawal, but the synthetic narcotic methadone has practical advantages over the real thing.

If the methadone dosage is not reduced, most heroin addicts adapt easily and completely to the new drug—they become methadone addicts. This hardly sounds like a solution to heroin addiction, but it is. For, unlike illegal heroin, methadone is a drug that can be lived with. It is reasonably safe. Since the drug is taken orally there is no danger of infection or needle shock. Overdosing is unlikely, because addicts do not develop tolerance to methadone which would require increased quantities of the drug. Most important, it provides no high. Methadone acts slowly, relieving withdrawal symptoms for up to twenty-four hours, but otherwise having little effect on the addict's mood, intelligence, or physical capacity.

Few methadone addicts seem inclined to go back to heroin. Well-run methadone programs manage to keep about 80 percent off smack for two years. For junkies who have never been arrested and who are not also alcoholics, the success rate is above 95 percent. And as a sort of social bonus, some methadone addicts manage to kick the drug habit completely. "Burn-out" is not an unheard-of phenomenon with heroin, but few heroin addicts who manage to survive the ten or twenty years before such a spontaneous change are in a position to rebuild their lives.

Legalize heroin. In the United States forty milligrams of heroin, a typical day's requirement, costs $20 to $100. In Great Britain, forty milligrams of heroin costs a nickel. The difference, of course, is that heroin is a legal drug in Britain, available by prescription from a clinic. Were the United States to adopt the British system, the annual cost of all the heroin used in the country would be less than five million dollars.

Legalizing heroin would save taxpayers and property owners billions, but would not eliminate addiction. This isn't a very important drawback to legalization, however, unless you believe there is some way to eliminate addiction completely. Decriminalizing heroin and reducing its price don't seem, on balance, to encourage addiction. Just one British citizen in fifty thousand takes heroin or morphine regularly, though possession has never been illegal. Another one in fifty thousand is on methadone maintenance. In the United States, one person in eight hundred is on junk.

These comparisons are sometimes dismissed as irrelevant, since conditions in the United States and England are so different. In fact, narcotics-dispensing clinics worked well in the United States from 1912 to 1924, serving twelve thousand addicts with maintenance doses of morphine. They were closed down only after an avalanche of propaganda from the Federal Bureau of Narcotics. And long after addicts were forced onto the streets of New York and Chicago and Los Angeles, physicians in Kentucky continued to prescribe morphine to users. The narcs chose to ignore this defiance of the law, fearing a constitutional test of the blanket narcotics ban, but the Kentucky experience is fascinating. Contrary to what might have been expected, the ease of obtaining drugs produced no increase in addiction.

Probably the only good reason not to legalize heroin is that it might attract addicts away from methadone. The case for legalization seems strong on balance, though, since some addicts are unwilling to stick with the synthetic. Besides, the disruptive influence of a narcotics habit is often exaggerated. Hundreds, perhaps thousands, of doctors are morphine addicts, yet continue to practice medicine undiscovered. Some experts believe that the kind of addict who does nothing but space out on heroin has far more serious problems that wouldn't go away after a switch to methadone or alcohol.

HOW TO EYEBALL A DIAMOND

Pliny the Elder—or so claims the American Gem Society—called diamonds "the most valuable of all things in this world." Nineteen hundred years later diamonds still fetch a pretty good price. A pound of gold costs about $3,000; a pound of good, gem-quality diamonds, cut and polished in one-carat chunks, is worth $2–$4 million. Fortunately, considerably less than a pound of diamonds is needed to make a splash. If you are in the market, weigh the following:

Diamond value. The wholesale price of a diamond is determined by its shape, color, clarity, and size. Shape is crucial to a gem's sparkle. A perfect "brilliant-cut" stone has precisely the proportions needed to reflect the maximum amount of light. To achieve these perfect dimensions, however, more of the gross weight of the average uncut diamond must be sacrificed. The typical cut stone has too broad a top facet and too "thin" a profile. When the error is substantial, the effect is noticeable without special equipment or lighting.

Very expensive diamonds are almost colorless. Otherwise similar stones marred by a visible dull yellow hue may be worth just one tenth as much. Most diamonds fall somewhere in between colorless and yellow, with prices to match. Note that an exception to this rule holds for so-called "fancy diamonds." These rare (and valuable) gems can be pink, yellow, red, green, or blue, and come in varying shades. Chances of seeing one in an ordinary jewelry store are remote. A diamond's color, incidentally, can be measured quite objectively by machine, then graded on one of several well-defined scales.

The clarity of a stone, its freedom from tiny crystalline imperfections, can't be measured so objectively, but experts usually produce identical ratings for the same diamond. A truly flawless diamond, one with no dark specks detectable under 10× magnification, sells at a substantial premium above stones with minor flaws. And not surprisingly, a diamond with a flaw visible to the naked eye is worth just a fraction of the price of a nearly flawless gem. Since it takes no special training to see flaws under magnification, use your dealer's microscope—not a jeweler's loop—to compare potential purchases.

Weight is the remaining component to the value of a diamond. For quality gems, value increases far more rapidly than size. A nearly colorless, nearly flawless half-carat stone is worth about $800, retail, while a stone three times as large runs close to $5,000. Price and weight are a matter of supply and demand. Large diamonds with few flaws are, by comparison, quite rare.

Buying diamonds. Since diamonds are graded uniformly by color, clarity, and size, it's possible to comparison-shop. Markups on small stones—less than a half carat—vary enormously, running as much as 100 percent. A neighborhood jeweler's $180 engagement ring might cost only $145 on sale at Sears. The gap between wholesale and retail prices shrinks to about 15 percent on big diamonds, though here the final price is often a matter of bargaining. Some retailers never bargain, but many will succumb to pressure when you make it clear you can go elsewhere.

Unless your jeweler's name is Cartier, it makes sense to have a large stone independently appraised before you plunk down your thousands. An appraisal, including a precise description of the gem, is also useful for insurance or resale. Remember that any reputable jeweler should be prepared to guarantee in writing the color, clarity, and weight of the diamond.

Investing in diamonds. If the idea is to own something beautiful, look around and find out what is really important to you. It probably doesn't make sense to pay two or three times as much for a flawless stone when the imperfections are invisible. Nor is it necessary to pay the premium for colorless gems. For that matter, the most sensible purchase of all may be a high-quality fake at $30 to $80 a carat. Machine-made imitations look very good, especially if kept clean and unscratched. They lack the brilliance of colorless diamonds, but few people can tell the difference without a genuine stone for comparison.

If the idea is to invest in diamonds as a hedge against inflation or as speculation, only large, very high-quality stones should be considered. It also makes sense to avoid gems with unusual shapes or colors. The market for such diamonds is particularly illiquid; should you be forced to sell quickly, you might recoup only half your investment.

The advantages of storing assets as diamonds are obvious. They are portable, virtually indestructible, and recognized as common currency anywhere in the world. During the last decade of inflation they have more than held their own with other precious commodities. Note, however, the disadvantages. The brokerage costs of diamonds (10–100 percent) are much higher than for securities or gold. Unless you hold diamonds for many years, the chances of coming out ahead are small. Moreover, the value of your diamonds is not determined by impersonal market forces. A South African cartel controls the supply, hence the price, of new gems entering the market. Judging from the cartel's past behavior, diamond prices are likely to keep pace nicely with inflation. But any serious windfalls to be had in diamonds will depend upon the active intervention of the cartel bosses.

HOW TO FIND A SAFE NEIGHBORHOOD

As you might expect, it's a lot easier to find places to avoid than spots where you'd risk a midnight stroll without a sidearm. According to the FBI, it's twice as likely you'll be murdered in a city than in a small town, six times as likely you'll be mugged. Rural areas have very low property-crime rates, but are catching up quickly in homicide and rape.

The most violent state in the Union in 1973 was New York, but other states took the honors in individual categories: homicide—Georgia (17.4 per 100,000), rape—Nevada (46 per 100,000), assault—North Carolina (337 per 100,000). North Dakota ranks safest on the same index, with an over-all violent-crime rate just one twelfth that of New York. Vermont, New Hampshire, Iowa, Maine, and Wisconsin trail behind, in that order. It's twenty-two times as likely, incidentally, you'll be murdered in Georgia than in North Dakota.

By traditional (and questionable) measurements, poor old New York City wins the violent-crime sweepstakes, ahead of such standbys as Baltimore, Los Angeles, Chicago, Miami, Las Vegas, Detroit, and San Francisco. These figures are a bit misleading, though, since the areas reporting in-

clude big chunks of suburbia in some cases, and don't account for the large visitor populations in others. Detroit is supposed to be the murder capital of the Western world, but the statistics say otherwise. Among large cities, Atlanta and New Orleans lead Motown by a nose. And surprisingly (to us, at least), residents of many smaller cities harm each other very, very frequently. Murder rates in Biloxi (19.7), Jackson, Mississippi (20.8), Jacksonville (19.8), Savannah (19.5), Waco (21.6), and Santa Cruz (20.3) all lead New York (17.5), Cleveland (15.1), and Houston (15.9).

By far the safest city over a million (including suburbs) is Milwaukee (murder—5.0, rape—16.6, assault—64.1). Going down the list, Indianapolis, Cincinnati, Buffalo, Minneapolis, San Diego, San Jose, and Pittsburgh all do well. Minneapolis had only 3.7 murders per 100,000 in 1973.

What you make of all this comes down to faith. A big problem with crime statistics is the way they lump together neighborhoods. If you live in Grosse Pointe, Michigan, how much does it matter that half of Detroit proper is killing the other half on Saturday night? Need the good citizens of Whitefish Bay, Wisconsin, fear the muggers who prowl downtown Milwaukee?

Statistics are also no better than the people who collect them. The FBI prints what police departments send them in the mail. Even if police are all equally conscientious, there's good reason to believe that the percentage of unreported crimes varies dramatically. A 1973 Census interview survey of big-city residents shows that 61 out of every 1,000 residents of "safe" Milwaukee were victims of violence, a full 70 per 1,000 in Minneapolis. Yet supposedly besieged Washingtonians admit just 31 violent crimes per 1,000, Miami just 22. . . .

Probably the only sure way to escape crime is to move out of the country. Israel records one third the murder rate of the United States (though there are other dangers), Japan just one fourth, England one eighteenth. Norway is the absolute champion among nations that publish. An average of 20 Norwegians are murdered each year, about one week's quota for Chicago.

HOW TO FOOL ALL THE PEOPLE SOME OF THE TIME

"So what you do is just reach up there and get that lever and just say, 'All the way with LBJ.'

"Your mamas and your papas and your grandpas, some of them are going to forget this. But I am depending on you young folks who are going to have to fight our wars, and who are going to have to defend this country, and who are going to get blown up if we have a nuclear holocaust— I am depending on you to have enough interest in your future and what is ahead of you to get up and prod mama and papa and make them get up early and vote."

—Lyndon B. Johnson
October 31, 1964

G HOW TO GET AN AUDIENCE WITH THE POPE

It's next to impossible to get a private audience with Pope Paul VI. Not only is the Pontiff aging, he is enormously busy. Private audiences are reserved for Church and religious leaders, heads of state, and occasional secular celebrities. Henry Kissinger stops in often on his way to Cairo or Damascus; less exciting but more frequent courtesy calls are the province of the U.S. Ambassador to Italy. Betty Friedan was among those Americans who did secure a private meeting recently—Ms. Friedan gave the Pope a medallion of the women's movement and he gave her a bronze religious medal.

For the rest of us, there are general audiences held most Wednesday mornings. Admission to general audiences is arranged in Rome through the Bishops' Office for U.S. Visitors to the Vatican. These audiences last about an hour and include hundreds, sometimes thousands, of pilgrims and travelers who meet in the new audience hall on the south side of St. Peter's, or, in summer, at the Pope's hot-weather retreat, Castel Gandolfo. Every year about 60,000 Americans make it to these general audiences—we're the best-represented nationality, after the Italians.

Plan ahead for admission to a general audience. Most visitors are announced to the Bishops' Office, and its head, the Reverend Eugene Walsh, O.S.M., by letters from their local bishops or pastors. Travel agents who include a papal audience in their tour of Rome also work through Father Walsh. It's possible, however, just to wander in off the street (the Via dell'Umiltà in downtown Rome) and apply to the Bishops' Office. Father Walsh submits a list to the Vatican every Friday for the next Wednesday's audience, and passes are issued through the office of the Prefecture of the Apostolic Household.

If you make it to a general audience, you'll hear the Pope speak, and perhaps shake his hand, or, if you are a Roman Catholic, kiss his ring. But if you don't, you can still get a glimpse of the Holy Father in the window of his Vatican apartment. He's there every Sunday he's in town, and at noon he waves and gives his traditional blessing to the crowd in the piazza.

HOW TO GET AWAY FROM IT ALL

The Scott Meadows Club offers a home far away from home in the case of nuclear attack, worldwide famine, or the election of Spiro Agnew. In return for an immodest down payment and modest dues, Scott Meadows will set aside your own family cabin on its 700-acre retreat somewhere in the High Sierras of California. The club's exact location is privileged information—guests are brought in blindfolded —to insure security in case of apocalypse.

HOW TO GET EVEN

They say revenge is a dish best eaten cold, but the most appropriate flavor is rarely specified. Pie-Kill Unlimited, the love generation's answer to Murder, Inc., currently offers a choice of lemon meringue or chocolate cream; other varieties on special order.

In case you've yet to hear of it, Pie-Kill is a business service which throws pies for a price. Frustrated by a furniture salesman who promised delivery six weeks ago? Tired of that table next to the kitchen door at La Grenouille? Had enough of a boss who thinks a nameplate on the door gives him license to lech? Instead of buying a gun, contact Pie-Kill (Suite 504, 152 West Forty-second Street, New York, New York 10036) and arrange for proper revenge, anonymity guaranteed. A 3,000-calorie bomb costs $50 to $100, depending on the accessibility of the victim. Classrooms, wide-open offices, and stores are ideal sites. Naturally, heavily buffered corporate execs and bureaucrats are extra. Should you prefer something more modest, a plain seltzer-water attack is also available.

HOW TO GET INTO A EUROPEAN
MEDICAL SCHOOL

Getting into medical school these days is about as difficult as borrowing for your funeral expenses, and it will get tougher. Pill pushing is very in. Something like half the freshpeople at good colleges are signing up for pre-law or pre-med programs. American medical schools are unwilling and perhaps unable to expand sufficiently to admit more than a fraction of the applicants who meet reasonable standards. If you are one of the majority who can't make the grade at Harvard or Marquette or Hahnemann, take heart. There remains a difficult, though perfectly legal way of becoming an M.D.: go to school abroad.

Medical schools in a number of countries accept Americans. The most popular destinations are the universities of Guadalajara in Mexico and Bologna in Italy. As of the early 1970's, in fact, just four U.S. medical schools had more Americans enrolled than Bologna.

Once you've finished all the requirements of the foreign institution, the remaining barrier to practicing in the United States is a standardized equivalency examination given by an American Medical Association surrogate called the Educational Council of Foreign Medical Graduates (ECFMG).

General considerations in choosing a foreign medical school:

Quality. The value of a foreign medical degree varies widely; officially because it may not get you past the ECFMG exam, unofficially because it may handicap your chances for a good hospital internship and residency. About half those taking the ECFMG fail to qualify, with Mexican medical graduates faring substantially worse than European. Since these statistics include everyone taking the exam, not just Americans, it would be foolish to make too much of these success ratios. Most observers still agree, however, that medical training in Northern European schools is superior to Southern European and Mexican. Note, too, that degrees from unaccredited schools don't even make you eligible to take the ECFMG. The World Health Organization (20 Avenue Appia, 1211 Geneva 27,

73

Switzerland) publishes a compendium, *The World Directory of Medical Schools*, listing schools which meet the minimum standard.

Entrance requirements. As variable as training standards. Schools in Switzerland, Germany, Belgium, the

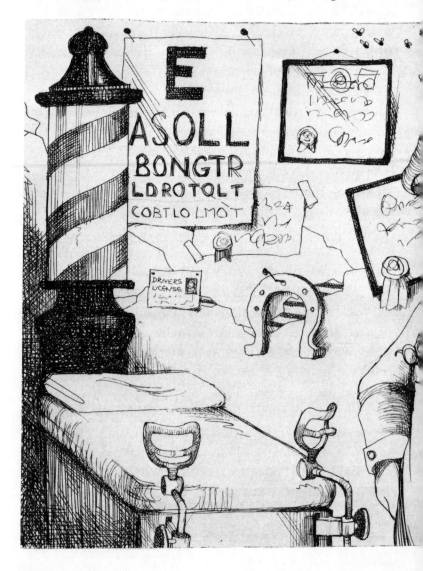

Netherlands, and France require roughly the same pre-med courses and level of academic excellence as less prestigious U.S. schools. Until recently, Spanish, Italian, and Mexican schools had relatively lax standards for foreigners willing to pay full tuition. Now, you'll probably need B-average

college grades. In some cases a competitive entrance exam is also used to cull the best applicants. Check with the consulate of each country for up-to-date facts on the application procedure. Remember, too, getting in doesn't guarantee you'll stay in. Unlike American schools, many foreign institutions feel no compulsion to help you make it through. If you just scraped by in college, chances are you will be wasting your time in medical school, no matter what the country.

Another major roadblock is, of course, language. Medical schools in English-speaking countries are as difficult to get into as American schools. Hence, there is no way to beat the problem, other than becoming fluent in the relevant language. Schools such as Bologna may make a few concessions to foreigners, but don't count on it.

Time. Going to a foreign medical school adds between one and three years to your time between college and private practice. The equivalent of med school and internship—the two are typically integrated—takes 5½ (Germany) to 7 years (Belgium), providing you pass all exams the first time around. Quite possibly an additional year of internship in a U.S. hospital will be necessary to meet state requirements when you return. Yet another potential snag is a government service requirement in the foreign country. As in the United States, fresh M.D.'s may face a year in the military after graduation. Don't plan on beating the system by transferring back to the United States after a few years abroad. Successful transfer applications are very rare.

Should you be short on initiative and long on cash, a medical-school placement service might help. They can't get you in if you don't meet the requirements of the foreign

university, but they can save you the bother of correspond-
ing with a dozen schools, plus the sometimes endless red
tape involved in dealing with bureaucracies.

One of these services, the Medical School Admissions
Center (102-30 Queens Boulevard, New York, New York)
claims to match fairly weak candidates with schools happy
to have more Americans. Matchmaking doesn't come cheap:
MSAC charges $250 for a consultation, another $750 to find
the right med school.

HOW TO GET ON A TV GAME SHOW

Not everyone can be Queen for a Day. But if you don't
mind dressing up like Steve Reeves in *Hercules Unchained*
—or if telling thirteen million viewers that your husband
prefers Big Macs to sex won't raise a blush to your cheeks—
you may have a future in television. Never before, not even
in the days of "$64,000 Question" and "The Big Surprise,"
have there been so many TV extravaganzas giving away so
much to so many. Game shows dominate daytime television
and have established a beachhead in prime time. Individual
prizes are smaller than during the Golden Age—at press
time, the CBS house limit was $25,000; ABC, $30,000—but
hundreds more are sharing in the wealth. One American
city, which shall remain anonymous, is entertained each day
by twenty-four shows.

The guiding force behind this cultural renaissance is the
Federal Communications Commission. First, to promote
regional diversity, the FCC turned over the 7:30–8:00 P.M.

slot to local stations. Instead of "Mod Squad" we got syndicated versions of "Hollywood Squares" and "The Price Is Right." Then, to reduce exposure of the young to vicarious violence, the FCC leaned on the networks to set aside 8:00–9:00 P.M. as "family hour." No doubt the result will be weekends in Rome for volunteers willing to mate with a porpoise in some Burbank studio. The networks, of course, are delighted. Weekends in Rome and rented porpoises are chicken feed, compared to the cost of fifty-two minutes of "Hawaii Five-O" or "Cannon."

To join in the festivities, you must first be a member of the studio audience. ABC suggests you write for tickets directly to the production company—producers are listed in the credits. For NBC's West Coast shows (that's virtually all of them), apply to NBC Tickets, 3000 West Alameda, Burbank, California 90515. For CBS New York shows, try the CBS Ticket Bureau, 524 West Fifty-seventh Street, New York, New York 10019; CBS Los Angeles—CBS Television City, 7800 Beverly Boulevard, Hollywood, California 90036. Once you're in the audience, the line forms on the right.

Producers like their contestants to be bright, attractive, and energetic, but not necessarily in that order. Your heavy shows—"Concentration," "Rhyme and Reason," "Password" —involve ad-libbing and an occasional display of wit. For most, though, enthusiasm is everything. Producers are looking for the contestant who'll swoon at the sight of a GE combination washer-dryer, jerk like a hooked trout for a belted Emba mink coat. Women seem to do better than men, but almost anyone can learn to radiate with practice.

If your grin isn't goofy enough for "Let's Make a Deal," your *joie de vivre* insufficient for "Money Maze," take consolation. Do you really want a GE combination washer-dryer or a belted Emba mink coat, anyway? One disillusioned winner from Brooklyn would like to know how to fit a redwood swimming pool with diving board into her studio apartment.

HOW TO GROW AN AVOCADO

When shopping, remember that larger, rougher, dark-skinned Florida avocados are usually better-behaved houseplants than the smaller California variety. Any kind of avocado will sprout and give forth leaves, however, if you allow it to germinate and plant it in decent soil. Sometimes roots start to sprout even before you get the pit out of the fruit. If so, wash the pit in warm water and proceed. If not, either peel it or just leave it in a warm place for a day or so until the skin dries up and falls off.

From here, there are two schools of thought on avocado culture. Some like to skewer the naked pit and suspend it in a glass of warm water on a tripod of toothpicks while the roots develop. This method allows supervision of root growth; it may amuse, but only postpones the day when you must bury the little darling.

It's faster then, and more efficient, just to plant the pit in a medium-sized pot (about six inches across will do for the first year) in a mix of two thirds potting soil and one third humus or garden dirt. Avocados prefer rich, loamy soil. Plant base (wider part) down, and cover about two thirds of the way up.

Then water frequently. With warm water, please. If your house is dry you may invert a clear cup over the pit to create a humid environment. Eventually it will split and germinate; almost every pit cooperates, but it may take up to three months, so be patient. Your avocado is busy underground.

Once sprouted, an avocado grows fast, a prime reason for its popularity with the brown-thumb set. The first shoot will be straight and tender. You must be cruel and determined. When the new stalk reaches six inches in height, snip it off halfway, straight across. The result will look miserable at first, but your clipped avocado seedling will fight back with new shoots and more leaves. Now you should bury the pit completely.

From here on, you are in charge. Feed the avocado often, keep it well watered, and prune in any direction you fancy. Unless you do prune it will follow a natural inclination to be tall and gawky, but ruthless shears can force it into a bushy globe. After a year or so, you will probably need to repot—the general rule is that a plant's height should not exceed the diameter of the pot by more than five times. New soil every two years is a good idea also.

Naming your avocado is strictly optional, but we feel it promotes healthy identification with weak, green things. . . .

HOW TO HAVE YOUR CAKE AND EAT IT TOO

Lytton Strachey, the British biographer and man of letters, was compelled to defend his conscientious objection to World War I before a military draft tribunal. Attempting to trap the pacifist, one of the inquisitors demanded to know what he would do if he saw a German soldier trying to violate his sister.

Strachey's reply: "I would try to get between them."

HOW TO HEDGE AGAINST INFLATION

Eat right, get plenty of sleep, and see your doctor for an annual checkup. The chemicals in your body, which sold for just 98 cents in 1936, are now worth $5.60.

HOW TO IMPROVE YOUR GOLF GAME

Forget about mail-order manuals; it's impossible to hold a book while you're trying to chip out of a sand trap, and embarrassing to ask the caddie to read it aloud. Country-club pros help a little bit, but we all know that the problem isn't so much athletic as it is attitudinal. To get

into the right spirit, join the Church of Perfect Liberty, a new Japanese import which teaches members both how to live right and how to cut their golf scores by five.

The Church claims an international membership of three million and owns eleven golf courses around the world. Converts may be found in Brazil, Britain, and France as well as Southern California, where CPL hopes to be teeing off sometime in 1976. Plans for a virtual golfers' paradise in the Malibu Mountains not far from Los Angeles have been slowed by an array of nonbelievers, most notably the Sierra Club. The Malibu site, it seems, is deep in backpackers' country, a combination of meadowland, hills, and streams. To which the Church of Perfect Liberty might say: different strokes for different folks.

HOW TO INCREASE YOUR HEIGHT

This is no joke. A study of University of Pittsburgh graduates in 1967 revealed that men over 6 feet 2 inches had starting salaries 12 percent greater than men under 6 feet. Even if you subtract the professional athletes from the sample, tall men did better than short men.

Should you need to be a little taller for just a few hours —say, to squeeze past a civil service physical—the solution is simple. An average adult is one half to one inch taller at the beginning of the day than at the end. During the day the spongy disks that separate the vertebrae in the spine slowly contract under pressure. Each night they regain shape. If you can't schedule the examination for the morning, the next-best thing is to stay flat on your back until the moment of truth. A more radical approach is to stretch your spine by placing your body in traction. Stretching works (for a few hours), but it is a mite dangerous to try on your own.

An alternative offering permanence is to change your posture. The spine is curved into an S shape. If you were to straighten it out, you would end up four inches taller. Now, a perfectly straight back would not be practical—were you to manage such a miracle, there would be no way to stand up. But reducing an unnecessarily exaggerated spinal curvature through exercise may add a full inch to your height.

We won't include the details here—any self-help book on back problems tells what to do—but the idea is simple enough. Exercise can teach you to tuck in your pelvis and flatten the cervical, lumbar, and dorsal regions of the spine. The catch, of course, is that the boring exercises must be done faithfully and won't work if you already have a good posture. Better, perhaps, to stick with the guaranteed success of platform shoes.

HOW TO JOIN THE DAR

It's not like signing up for the Jaycees, you know. To make the grade you must (a) be a female over eighteen, (b) descend from a genuine American Revolutionary, (c) prove your parents were married at the time you were born, and (d) balance a teacup on your knee well enough to gain the endorsement of two members in good standing.

Before practicing up your teacup act, be advised that the Daughters take things very seriously. A WASPy name, sensible shoes, and a fear of socialism do not constitute evidence of eligibility. The Society has been especially vigilant since discovering that one prominent member—the regent of a local chapter—was actually the descendant of a wicked Tory.

Acceptable proof consists of a notarized pedigree (submitted in duplicate) of descent from a Revolutionary figure. The pedigree must be built from legal records, wills, cemetery inscriptions, and printed genealogies. For each ancestor in your pedigree you must be able to supply at least two of three vital dates (birth, death, marriage) and probable date of the third.

Getting back to 1776 is only half the fun. An exact census of patriots will never be known, since the Revolution predates the FBI. The DAR does publish its own index (105,000 names) of Continental Congresspeople, tea-partygoers, registered Army vets, prisoners of war, preachers against the Crown, munitions makers, and persons who paid substitutes to go to war in their place. Descent from anyone on the list is good enough for the ladies.

Questions? Write the National Society, Daughters of the American Revolution, 1776 D Street, N.W., Washington, D.C. 20006.

HOW TO KEEP A PIPE LIT

Ask a pro, like William Vargo of Swartz Creek, Michigan. By virtue of keeping 3.3 grams (about one tenth of an ounce) of cube-cut burley tobacco lit continuously for 1 hour, 37 minutes, and 27 seconds, Mr. Vargo won the 1974 World Pipe Smoking Contest. That, by the way, is 27 minutes, 40 seconds shy of the all-time record in International Association of Pipe Smokers' Clubs (IAPSC) competition, set in 1954 by Max Igree of Flint, Michigan.

Endurance techniques vary, with experts split between the even-surface burn and slow-spreading corner burn. Corner-burn types must accept the risk of early flame-out—rules prohibit relighting after the first sixty seconds of a contest. Tamping, to maintain high density, is, of course, accepted practice.

One foreign technique—starting with less than a full 3.3-gram load and adding to the bowl as time passes—can generate spectacular results. Using the gradual-fill method, Yrje Pentikainen of Finland kept his pipe alight for 4 hours, 11 minutes, 28 seconds. IAPSC officials disallow this alien technique and point out that Pentikainen employed stringy, slow-burn tobacco, rather than regulation cube-cut.

HOW TO KEEP UP WITH
FAST-BREAKING NEWS

United Press International has an information service, called the Special Washington Wire, which is subscribed to by many businesses. UPI says that they will also sell the service to individuals. The Special Washington Wire gives national, international, and business news of general interest as it happens; the word comes over a teletype machine (an electronic Extel printer) that can be installed in your home or office. It's a small, compact machine about the size of a portable typewriter. The monthly rental is $245 (minimum contract, twelve months) and includes a supply of teletype paper. Contact UPI at 220 East Forty-second Street, New York.

The Associated Press has a similar service, but their representative said he thought it would be in bad taste to tell us about it.

HOW TO LEAVE THE HOSPITAL IN BETTER SHAPE THAN YOU ENTERED

Medical historians like to argue about when it first made sense to be treated in a hospital. The consensus is sometime in the late nineteenth century. Before then, the chances of contracting someone else's disease were greater than the chances that primitive drugs or surgical techniques could make you well.

Medicine marches on. The art of healing has advanced, but the odds of catching something nasty in a hospital are still distressingly high. Your greatest risk is from a blood or plasma transfusion. Both whole blood and the pale-yellow fluid component of blood called plasma carry hepatitis viruses if the donor ever had the disease. Every year 30,000 patients contract serum hepatitis from transfusions; about 3,000 of them never leave the hospital alive.

The major sources of deadly blood are commercial blood farms, private enterprises which buy blood and plasma from skid-row bums or whoever walks in the door. There is no

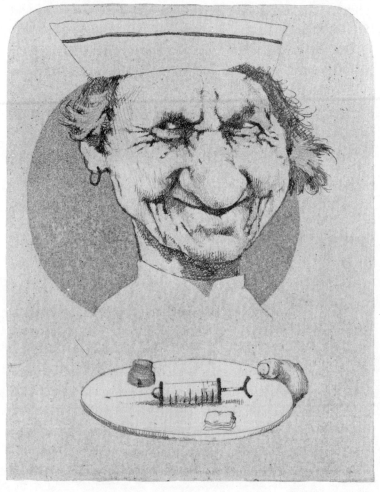

100 percent effective test for the presence of dormant hepatitis viruses, so there would be no way for a conscientious commercial blood collector to screen out all offending donations. And besides, few blood farms have a conscience.

It is possible to insist—do it in writing to your physician, with a copy to the hospital—on receiving Red Cross volunteers' blood. The hospital will probably comply. If they don't, they may be liable to a malpractice suit. The problem is that volunteers' blood is not completely free of hepatitis, either. Sometimes the disease goes undiagnosed, so victims with the best intentions can pass on the virus. Countries which have no commercial blood sales have also faced the hepatitis plague.

Hence, your only certain protection is to demand (in writing) that the hospital substitute synthetic plasma expander for the real thing whenever medically feasible. Plasma expander is just sterile salt solution. In most cases, it performs the main task of plasma or whole-blood transfusions, adding liquid volume to bring blood pressure back to normal. Using plasma expander may slow recovery by a day or two—the organic components of natural plasma must be regenerated. But the insurance is worth that price. And as a bonus, you save money. Hospitals nail you for plasma at the rate of $50 to $100 a pint. Plasma expander is just clean salt water.

HOW TO LIE DOWN WITH THE DEVIL

Faced with declining membership, the Order of the Most Holy Trinity was able to attract little attention with notices in standard religious media. An ad in *Playboy*, however, brought forth six hundred applicants.

HOW TO LOSE WEIGHT IN STYLE

Tired of broccoli and broiled chicken dinners? Too smart to fall for the low-carbohydrate, high-fat route to hardened arteries? Too lazy to jog five miles a day? You are in luck—there really is a better way.

Just set aside two weeks (and a few thousand dollars) to make the pilgrimage to Eugénie-les-Bains (write 40320 Geaune), a tiny town in south-central France. Eugénie-les-Bains is the site of a splendid resort hotel, Les Prés d'Eugénie, offering its guests all the standard luxuries—restored Belle Epoque interiors, tennis, indoor and outdoor pools, manicured gardens. But what makes Les Prés so special is its dining room, the only great French restaurant in the world dedicated to dieters.

The genius behind this enterprise is Michel Guérard, one of the new breed of French chefs whose style is marked by simplicity and restraint. Guérard became famous in the late 1960's as the proprietor of Le Pot au Feu, a bistro tucked between grimy warehouses in a Parisian suburb. *Foie gras* and wild raspberries in such a dismal setting proved irresistible to France's jaded food aristocracy; Le Pot au Feu remained everyone's best undiscovered restaurant until it fell prey to urban renewers in 1973.

Rather than reopen in a more accessible neighborhood, Guérard chose to move operations to Eugénie. His own weight problem and the desires of the clientele—Eugénie is an old mineral-water spa where cityfolk traditionally come to pay their dues—inspired the new dieters' menu. The three-course lunches and dinners (about $10) never contain more than 500 calories, yet never give the slightest hint of compromise. Exactly how Guérard does it is a trade secret, but some of the tricks are fairly transparent. Butter, flour, and sugar have been banished; sauces are enriched with finely blended low-fat cheeses. Meats, fish, and vegetables are all super-fresh and sparingly cooked.

A couple of weeks of Guérard's painless regime, combined with tennis and swimming, should knock off from five to ten pounds—plenty to cover a year's worth of surplus martinis and Sara Lee. If your ambitions are more modest, ponder the following: Guérard maintains a separate menu for the unweight-conscious, a menu every bit as wonderful as the one at the old Pot au Feu. Hence it's possible to diet at lunch and gorge at dinner. There are worse ways to spend a vacation.

HOW TO MAKE A COMPOST HEAP

Yes, you too can shred your way to better soil. All that's needed is an isolated corner in the backyard or a sheltered area behind a hedge or garage, and neighbors who don't mind .an occasional whiff when the wind turns.

Composting consists of mixing solid organic wastes together in the proper way and allowing them to decompose. Natural chemical processes, carried out by a host of micro-organisms (bacteria, molds, and the like) and small animals (beetles, bugs, worms), turn garbage into gold. Well, maybe not gold, but at least fertilizer.

First things first: the word "heap" is a misnomer. For best results, compost materials should not be tossed together haphazardly, but should be laid down in well-planned layers in a convenient place near a source of water. If you want to build your compost heap with assorted forms of crud as they come available, you must mix them thoroughly. Fine materials become matted easily and prevent adequate air circulation; coarse materials take longer to decay. For best results, layers of organic wastes should form the heap in proportions such as:

1. three to six inches of straw, leaves, weeds, garbage (the carbon source),
2. an inch of manure, fertilizer, or any nitrogen-rich material,
3. an inch or two of topsoil, wood ashes, eggshells (the calcium source),
4. a fine sprinkling of lime to cut the stink and reduce acidity.

Repeat this scheme until the pile is three to five feet high.

The optimum size for a compost heap is five to ten feet wide and no more than five feet high. Smaller, suburban compost bins, housed in garbage cans or wooden barrels, work well if space is limited. Where winters are tough and summers dry, make compost heaps in foot-deep pits. In temperate climates, fall is the best time to start—plant wastes are plentiful and the finished muck will be ready for spring.

Shredding is the key to your quick compost. It increases the total surface area of the raw organic material, thereby speeding fermentation. The faster compost is made, the more valuable it is for your soil because there is less time for the dissipation of gases and leaching out of essential elements.

What to shred? Almost any organic material is eligible. Use kitchen garbage: raw vegetable and fruit peelings, coffee grounds, tea leaves, nutshells, corncobs, or any kind of table scraps. Recycle lawn clippings, hair clippings, sawdust, leaves, newspapers, anonymous sludge. Empty the vacuum-cleaner bag into the pile. Good natural nitrogen sources include manure, bone, soybean or cottonseed meal. Should you lack a home source for such, try a garden-supply store.

Some composters get in trouble by using too much of a single ingredient. If you use only leaves, weeds, or grass clippings, for instance—all good carbon sources—nothing much will happen. Even a small addition of nitrogen-rich material will make the difference. Nitrogen, which nourishes the compost bacteria, should be present in a carbon-nitrogen ratio of between 15:1 and 30:1; convenient household compost materials often fall out of this range.

Aeration is also essential for a speedy compost. The goal

is to create a happy home for guest insects and miscellaneous smaller organisms to carry out the job. Initially, every three or four days is not too often to turn the material. To find out exactly when to meddle, thrust a thermometer into the center of the pile. It's ready when the temperature hits 150 degrees. Wastes that aren't yet fully decayed should be worked toward the center. If you are using a container or bin, aerate frequently, and remember to leave openings for drainage. Cognoscenti place wooden poles at intervals throughout the heap, or plant them vertically, to be pulled out later for aeration channels.

Especially at the start, it's important to keep the compost quite moist, but don't become too zealous. The best degree of moisture is that of a wrung-out sponge, not wet enough to squeeze water out, yet damp to the touch. For best results, distribute the finished compost annually in sheets one to three inches thick.

Bon appétit!

HOW TO MAKE AN OMELET WITHOUT BREAKING EGGS

Communiqué from the Red Guerrilla Family to the people of San Francisco, July 29, 1975:

On Monday, July 21, a bomb detonated in the Tishman Building on Market Street in San Francisco before the building was fully evacuated, even though we had made a 25-minute warning giving the time, place, and magnitude of the explosion. At 9:37 we phoned the Associated Press. We told them that the bomb would go off at 10:00. We also told them that

the bomb was very powerful, and that the building and the streets around it should be cleared. Asked if they understood our warning, the AP said they did. At 9:50 we repeated this warning to an operator.

We don't know why nobody warned the workers in the building. Either the AP, the police, or the building guards, whether deliberately or through confusion, failed to order a full evacuation. . . .

We hope that the media share our concern for the lives of the people. We would like the media to study these simple suggestions on what to do when a bomb warning is received. Everyone who answers a telephone should understand them:

1. Get the time and place of the explosion, and any special

95

instructions on what must be done to clear the area. Get the facts straight the first time we say them. You can do other detective work later.

2. Phone the police as soon as we hang up.

3. Try to phone the building as well.

THE MOST IMPORTANT THING IS TO RELAY THE WARNING AS QUICKLY AS POSSIBLE. Even if we have already phoned the police and the building ourselves, the media's confirmation of the warning can only help.

We apologize to the workers in the Tishman Building whose lives were put in danger. We are very glad none of you were seriously hurt.

We make these bombs as safe as possible from accidental detonation. We are not going to use any anti-disturbance devices if there is any chance that a worker might find a bomb. We would like to recommend these steps to workers who find suspicious objects:

1. Don't handle anything suspicious. If you have picked it up, put it down without tipping it.

2. Warn all your comrades on that floor or in the area.

3. Leave the area. If you are in a multi-story building, and you do not know when the bomb will detonate, use the stairs, not the elevators.

4. Tell the building guards. Phone the police. Have them clear the entire building.

5. Do not stand right outside the building. Be careful to pick a spot where the glass can't fall on you.

6. Nobody, including the bomb squad, should be allowed to handle the device until the building has been fully evacuated.

We fully understand the questions people have asked about our evacuation procedure in this action. We feel that the underground is responsible to the people. We will continue to study ways to assure the safety of all workers and innocent people during actions, and we are open to suggestions.

We hope that the media will also make an effort to understand why this warning wasn't acted upon, so that we can prevent such a thing from happening again.

HOW TO MAKE A SILK PURSE

Former Treasury Secretary and Chairman of Democrats-for-Nixon John Connolly looks on the bright side. After his acquittal on bribery charges Connolly allowed that he might still be able to run for national political office. If the IRS, FBI, and Special Watergate Prosecutors couldn't pin anything on him following eighteen months of investigation, Connolly argued, he must be the most innocent politician in America.

HOW TO MIX A GREAT MARTINI

In this cruel world, the martini drinker is surely among the most ill-used. Magazine ads and liquor-store leaflets, transgressing all rules of decent human conduct, promote such perversions as the white-rum martini and the martini with bitters. Otherwise civilized hosts press odd mixtures of vodka and vermouth upon helpless guests. Expensive restaurants offer 8o-proof bar gin, the kind meant only to be disguised in gimlets.

Some of these abuses must be chalked up to parsimony. How else to explain the Harvard Club's policy—quickly rescinded after a torrent of protest—of adding one part vermouth to every *two* parts gin? Yet for others, deviations are better explained by ignorance. The classic martini no more needs improvement than the Moonlight Sonata. Only fine, high-proof gin is acceptable. Purists take sides on brands, though, in our view, any one of a number will do nicely—Bombay, Beefeater, Boodles, Tanqueray. The list of dry vermouths is shorter; we see no reason to go beyond Boissière or Noilly Prat. The proper ratio of gin to vermouth is 10:1. Much more gin and it won't taste like a martini. Much less and the sugar in the vermouth will clash with the gin flavoring.

Questions of garnish are complex. The twist of lemon has gained in popularity both because it masks second-rate gin and because it will do less damage than an olive or pickled onion. If you know the gin will be good, pass by the twist. If not, prudence dictates its inclusion. The fad of adding a slice of raw mushroom is harmless. Mushroom imparts no taste to the martini, though the martini does improve the flavor of the mushroom.

Of greater consequence is the issue of how to chill the mixture. James Bond made much of stirring versus shaking. We applaud author Fleming's attention to detail—especially since it reduced the number of dreary paragraphs on King and Country in each novel—but the very best martinis are made from gin and vermouth pre-chilled in a freezer. How to keep the potion cold once it is poured is a genuine matter of taste. The traditional martini is served straight up, preferably in a chilled glass. Lovely to look at, but must be drunk quickly. Of course, the martini on the rocks, or on cracked ice, stays cold longer. The inevitable dilution may be small price to pay if the alternative is warm gin.

Certain martini drinkers have hit upon a technological solution: the artificial ice cube. Hollow cubes filled with water, then sealed and frozen. As for us, we'll switch to rye and ginger before succumbing to gin on plastic.

HOW TO OBTAIN A DIVORCE FOR UNDER $100

The key, of course, is to avoid lawyers. Equally essential, you must arrange a truce with your spouse. A noncontested divorce is just a piece of paper, but a divorce with complications is a painful, costly business.

How painful and how costly depends upon the stamina and dollar value of the couple involved. In most states, $2,500 is the bare minimum spent by people in the $25,000–$50,000 income range—twice that if you can't agree on who keeps the Picasso ceramic, three times that if there's a custody fight. In California, legal costs run double those anywhere else, which is probably why the notion of the divorce kit was born in Lotus Land.

Divorce kits are an outgrowth of no-fault divorce—the idea that divorce is really nobody's business but the unhappy couple's. No-fault is now legal in all but a few states, and its major advantage is speed. Even with no-fault, however, the care and feeding of a lawyer will set you back plenty.

Do-it-yourself divorce kits, on the other hand, can be very cheap. A privately marketed "self-divorce" kit sells in Oregon—complete with forms and advice—for $25. (Filing fees are extra.) Similar kits have surfaced in Florida and Michigan, though not without some rumblings about their legality from the friendly neighborhood Bar. In California's Contra Costa County, self-divorce can be done via the U.S. Postal Service—filing fees and affidavits by the two parties

are mailed to the court. The judge decides if the parties need appear, and when there is no question of alimony and property division seems equitable, the court may grant the divorce by return post.

A divorce kit advertised in New York State sells for $98, including forms and instructions, but tops the limit with court costs of about another $100. New Yorkers seeking cheap divorces might consult *How to Get a New York Divorce for Under $100* by C. M. Allen, privately printed but widely available. Allen, who shows how to do it for $97.11 including sales tax, gives specific advice—names and addresses—and establishes beyond doubt that a non-lawyer who wants to can generate all the paper shuffling required for his or her own divorce.

Feminists seeking divorce might try *Women in Transition: A Feminist Handbook on Separation and Divorce* (Scribner's, $6.95). Written by a collective of Philadelphia women, it offers counsel and support as well as specifics on doing-it-yourself for cheap.

HOW TO OPEN A SWISS BANK ACCOUNT

It's easy as pie. There is no law against buying Swiss francs, then depositing them in a checking or savings account at a Swiss bank. Most banks require a minimum deposit, usually just $1,000. In the past, the Swiss government has also put ceilings on nonresident deposits, but for the moment this is not a problem.

Among the several hundred private Swiss banks ready to serve foreign accounts, a half dozen are particularly convenient since they have offices or representatives in the United States. These include the Swiss Credit Bank (New York, Los Angeles), the Union Bank of Switzerland (New York), and the Swiss Bank Corporation (New York, San Francisco, Los Angeles).

One hybrid of the standard Swiss account is a Swiss-franc deposit in a bank outside the borders of Switzerland. Swiss controls designed to discourage foreigners naturally don't apply—no limit on account size, no interest ceiling, no withholding taxes on earnings. The Bankhaus Deak in Vienna solicits such franc savings accounts, and pays high interest rates to boot. Their New York office (Deak International, 763 United Nations Plaza) will provide details and the necessary forms. A similar deal can be worked with Lloyds International Bank, but customers must apply in London.

Perhaps a better question than "how to" is "why" open a Swiss bank account. The payoff is supposed to be security and privacy. Certainly Swiss banks are unlikely to default on their deposit liabilities. But then neither are American banks protected by the Federal Deposit Insurance Corporation. The Swiss franc is one of the world's most stable currencies because the Swiss are willing to pay virtually any price to avoid inflation. As financial conservatives are only too happy to tell you, the value of the Swiss franc, measured against that of the American dollar, has increased by about 40 percent in the last five years.

This does not mean, though, that Swiss francs can never depreciate against the plain old dollar. Many economists believe that the dollar is a great bargain in foreign currency markets, suggesting that betting on further franc appreciation is, at best, risky.

Swiss banks are justly famous for guarding the privacy of their depositors. Whether or not you request the protection of a numbered account, as a matter of good business and government policy your secrets will be safe from credit agencies, corporate spies, and the like. On the other hand, the secrecy laws will not save you from the FBI or IRS, if it can be shown you have used the account to hide activities that are illegal under Swiss law. Hiding shady transactions from the SEC is O.K. Committing fraud—as Edith Irving discovered—is not. Should you decide to use an account for extralegal purposes, deal directly with the bank in Switzerland. Branches of Swiss banks in the United States must report large transactions to the Feds.

Balancing the legendary virtues of Swiss accounts are some less heralded vices. Let's assume you live and work in the United States. That means you pay rent and grocery bills in dollars. If you earn dollars, convert them to francs for safekeeping, and then reconvert them back to dollars for spending, the round trip will cost 1 or 2 percent in foreign-exchange fees. In addition, Swiss savings accounts pay lower interest rates than their American counterparts; it's probable you will lose 2–3 percent a year this way. If you have a large account, the financial penalties are even more dramatic. To discourage speculators, the Swiss ban any interest payments on foreign-owned accounts over 50,000 francs. They have also been known to tax these large accounts as much as 12 percent a year during speculative runs against the dollar and pound.

HOW TO OUTSMART A CHEESE SOUFFLÉ

This soufflé is an idiot's delight because there are no temperamental egg whites to beat.

SUSAN PREVIANT LEE'S VOILÀ CHEESE SOUFFLÉ

    4 eggs, extra large
    1⅓ cups heavy cream
    1 cup cheddar cheese, grated, lightly packed
    1 cup Parmesan, grated, lightly packed
    1 cup Gruyère, grated, lightly packed
    salt, pepper, dash of Worcestershire sauce, to taste

Combine eggs and cream in a large bowl and beat slightly with a fork. Add all the cheeses and the seasonings and beat again for a few minutes or until everything is combined. Pour into a large, 3-quart soufflé dish—don't butter the sides—and bake in a preheated oven. Start the oven at 450 degrees for 10 minutes and then lower to 400 degrees for about 35–40 minutes. Soufflé will puff up, brown at the top, but be almost creamy when cut into. *Voilà!*

    Serves 4.

HOW TO PICK AN AIRLINE

PRemember when it was fun to fly? It never really was, of course, but then we also once thought Sandra Dee was sexy and Lincoln Continentals had class. Pastel exteriors didn't make the seats any wider on Braniff 707's; flying Cheryl or Darleen to Miami didn't improve the food on National. The only fun thing about flying is getting there in reasonable comfort, on time, and in one piece.

When it comes to picking an airline, the industry and its regulators work hard to insure you have as little choice as possible, but they haven't succeeded completely:

Safety. All airlines in the United States are very safe. The majority of the trunk-line carriers—Continental, American, Northwest, Braniff, and Western—haven't had a single fatality in the last five years. You are twenty times more secure in a 747 at 30,000 feet than in the backseat of an Impala on the Pennsylvania Turnpike. Crashes are so rare that, if there is a difference among the big carriers in maintenance or pilot expertise, the statistics wouldn't show it.

Nitpickers, however, might wish to avoid portions of very long east-west routes. As a matter of personal convenience, plane crews often elect to fly through a dozen or more time zones in a few days. Hence a Pan Am pilot circling the globe in a week accumulates enough jet lag to impair the judgment of an ordinary mortal for a month. No one has proved that jet lag ever caused a crash, but you may not wish to wait until the first time.

The same nitpickers would be wise to consider the kind of aircraft they're flying. Every brand in the air is safe, though some may be safer than others. Wide-body jets—DC-10's, 747's, Lockheed 1011's—are loaded with modern guidance equipment and redundant control systems, but are potentially more vulnerable to explosive decompression from blown hatches, collisions, or bombs. The FAA has, in fact, ordered manufacturers of the jumbos to beef up the frames of the planes already in service; the recall may or may not be complete by the time you read this.

Rear-engined jets prized for their efficiency and interior quiet—727's, DC-9's, BAC-111's—may also have an inherent design problem. Some critics charge that they are more likely to catch fire on crash landing, since the fuel lines from wing tanks to engines are easily ruptured.

Economy. The airlines don't believe in competition, and neither do the federal bureaucrats who keep them in business. On occasion, as in the closest of families, disagreements do arise. Hence the infrequent price wars over youth fares, advance-payment discounts, no-frills anti-gimmicks. When a real maverick tries to shake things up, though, like World Airways' proposed $89 New York–Los Angeles tariff, the Old Boys close ranks. The only genuine bargains come from airlines which escape Civil Aeronautics Board scrutiny altogether, carriers operating routes entirely in one state. PSA in California leads the way with rock-bottom fares. Texas' Southwest does even better, letting customers choose between cut-rate fares and bonus fifths of Chivas Regal.

IATA, the international cartel promoted by our CAB to protect us from "destructive competition," has things sewed up just as tightly. Icelandic charges less than the cartel fare, but only on flights to Luxembourg. To obtain landing rights in London and Scandinavian airports, they

agreed to maintain the monopoly price on routes with direct competition. The only bright spot on the horizon is a proposal by Laker Airlines, a huge British charter group, to run a no-reservations, pack-'em-in-like sardines New York–London airbus. The CAB, to date, has simply ignored the application.

Comfort. To prevent "confusion," leg and shoulder room are carefully negotiated by the airlines. Now that the CAB has also nixed the scandalous coach lounges, the only real differences between lines are in types of aircraft and load factors.

Besides being less claustrophobic, jumbo jets have wider

seats and a bit more room to stretch. 747's provide an un-matchable feeling of spaciousness, while DC-10's and 1011's have more two-abreast seats. Probably as significant, the jumbos all have overhead compartments for carry-on lug-gage, a feature that saves you from hours of involuntary yoga exercises. The overhead compartments are so popular that many airlines have caved in and equipped their smaller planes with them, too.

The true airline aficionado knows, however, that the kind of airplane is less important than the percentage of seats that are filled. Every ride across the Atlantic shares food steamed in a common kitchen and identical 75-cent Dewar's miniatures. But the availability of service, the length of the lavatory lines, and the chances of sitting next to an empty seat vary dramatically. In 1974, 72 percent of the economy-class seats on El Al were taken, just 46 percent on Finnair. The American-flag carriers, TWA and Pan Am, averaged 54 percent full, while Air France, Lufthansa, Sabena, British Airways, Irish, and SAS filled about 65 percent of their seats. The differences are partly due to where the planes go—London is a more popular destination than Helsinki. When you have a chance, though, it pays to ride TWA, Pan Am, Alitalia, Air-India, Olympic, and Finn-air. So few people traveled British Caledonian and Japan Airlines that they quit the route altogether. One advantage, incidentally, that Pan Am, British Airways, and Air France share over all the others: daylight flights to Europe.

Comparisons of domestic passenger-load factors don't mean as much because of variations in routes. For the record, however, you are more likely to suffer a full cabin on American, Eastern, United, or Delta than on Northwest, Braniff, Continental, or TWA. Among the local airlines, Allegheny, Air West, Piedmont, and Southern are much more successful at stuffing their planes than North Central, Texas International, and Ozark.

On-time performance. To the CAB, "on time" means within fifteen minutes of the schedule. The latest data we saw (summer 1975) show Western leading the pack with 90 percent success. TWA, American, and United were not far behind. Northwest, Delta, and National score worst among trunk lines, averaging about 80 percent on time. The best rule of thumb is to avoid continuation flights. A Pittsburgh–Philadelphia flight originating in Pittsburgh has a better chance of leaving at the scheduled hour than a Pittsburgh–Philadelphia flight originating in Chicago. Worst of all are the legs of international flights, like the Seattle–Detroit portion of a Northwest flight from Tokyo.

HOW TO PICK A CARIBBEAN ISLAND

The inexorable march of the Holiday Inn, followed closely by the frozen veal Parmesan entrée and sullen servant, is leveling differences between Caribbean islands. Some modest versions of Paradise are still out there, however, provided you know what you are looking for. Herewith a checklist:

Tranquillity. A rarer commodity than the travel-agent hype would lead you to believe, unless you are willing to pay the price in basic amenities, hours (and dollars) spent getting there, and the like. San Andrés, a twenty-square-mile dot all by itself in the western Caribbean off the coast of Nicaragua, fits the description well. For the moment, it is very, very quiet, save during Christmas and Easter holiday weeks, when 500 or so Colombians fly up from Bogotá.

Closer and somewhat more convenient, the British Virgin Islands manage to absorb 50,000 tourists a year without fanfare. A half dozen of the 50 islands have hotel facilities ranging from spartan to super-luxurious. Other possibilities include Anguilla and Montserrat in the British West Indies, and a whole bunch of the Bahama Out Islands. Among the latter, Eleuthera and Abaco are moderately built up; the long string of little Out Islands (Inagua, Cat Island, San Salvador, etc.) are about as peaceful as you can find and just a few hundred miles from Miami.

Action. The sanitized variety, Las Vegas style, can best be found in Puerto Rico. Lots of noise, Latin beauties with feathers, rum drinks in hollow pineapples, roulette wheels. Like to gamble with the silk-suit, white-on-white, bulge-under-the-armpit crowd? Try Freeport or Aruba. If you can convince the high rollers you have a sincere desire to lose big, they'll even fly you down for free. Haiti offers its sin—the usual casinos and nightclubs, unusual brothels—with less Anglo-Saxon guilt than any other island.

Luxury. All the major islands have a few hotels with comfortable beds, reasonable soundproofing, and air conditioning that works. Real luxury is pretty scarce. Sint Maarten has the Oyster Pond Yacht Club and Caravanserai, both unflashily elegant and isolated from the island bustle.

St. Martin, the French side of the island, has another fine resort, La Samanna, which is equally isolated but less diffident about displaying its *luxe*.

Jamaica also manages a sprinkling of fine hotels. Frenchman's Cove, opulent and super-expensive, is so spacious that you hardly need meet the other guests. For the right price it's possible to have a bungalow and pool of your very own. The Jamaica Inn, Round Hill, and the Stony Hill Spa are all five-star, European-style resorts, specializing in perfect service.

Every hotel in the Rockresorts group is first-rate. Little Dix Bay (British Virgin Islands) and Caneel Bay (St. John) are in the low-key mold, while the Dorado Beach and Cerromar Beach in Puerto Rico are bigger and livelier, like good Florida Gold Coast hotels (assuming there could be a good Florida Gold Coast hotel). The latter two permit both children and conventions, not exactly a luxury feature unless you are a child or a conventioneer.

Economy. Caribbean prices drop incredibly as the precious winter sun turns to common summer humidity. At any season, however, you'll find what bargains there are to be had on the islands still building up their tourist business. Both the Dominican Republic and Haiti are currently fairly cheap, though neither has the standard Caribbean beaches or water sports. Trinidad and Tobago do have good beaches as well as first-class hotel rooms under $30 a day in high season. The Mexican islands Cancún and Cozumel can't match those prices, but are fair value. Cancún is brand-new, so new in fact that the construction mess could outweigh friendly hotel rates. Jamaica, generally an expensive island, has a number of older, more modest inns which are bargains. So do a few islands off the beaten path: St. Vincent, Carriacou (in the Grenadines), the Bahama Out Islands.

No matter how cheap the resort is, remember the advantage can be wiped out by air fares. This gives the edge to closer islands, particularly those with direct flights from the United States. The Bahamas are almost within swimming distance of Miami; Trinidad and Barbados are a full two hours farther by jet.

Diversions. If lying on your back under a coconut palm and stuffing your face with Caribbean lobsters doesn't make you happy, there are alternatives. Snorkeling and skin diving are great in the clear shallow waters off the Bahamas, notably on the Out Islands that haven't been used heavily. Other candidates include Tobago, Cozumel, the Grenadines, and the British Virgin Islands. The ultimate macho sport, deep-sea fishing, is possible just about anywhere in the Caribbean, but the boats to take you out are most easily available in Puerto Rico, the Bahamas, and Jamaica.

Caribbean golf courses are almost as common as Caribbean sand fleas. Really demanding courses, however, can be found in Puerto Rico (Dorado Beach, El Conquistador), the Dominican Republic (La Romana), and Jamaica (Runaway Bay). Tennis is the current "in" sport; all the new hotels have courts. Compulsive achievers will find teaching pros and plenty of competition in the U.S. Virgin Islands and Puerto Rico.

The straight tourism bit is unrewarding on most islands, with a few big exceptions. Cancún and Cozumel are a few miles off the coast of the Yucatán Peninsula, just a couple of hours from the great Mayan ruins at Uxmal and Chichén

Itzá. If you can see beyond the omnipresent poverty, the decadent ruin of Haiti is also quite a sight. Elsewhere, eschew the local cultural highlights unless you are particularly fond of third-rate colonial architecture, second-rate mountain vistas, and first-rate slums.

Weather. This is a phony issue, as far as our researches show. The weather isn't the same everywhere at any one time, but there is no pattern to speak of. The Bahamas do stand apart from the real Caribbean, suffering cool winters. Suitable for lying about or playing golf; generally too chilly to swim four months each year.

Otherwise the differences are apparently minor. Summers are six or seven degrees warmer than winters, with more rain in September, October, and November, the tropical-storm season. Nowhere are you likely to encounter four straight days of clouds, unless you carry them with you.

HOW TO PICK A PERFECT BRIE

We don't mean those metal tins of white-walled rubber tire so maliciously labeled Brie. Admittedly worse things can happen to cheese than canning and pasteurization—indignities like being suffused with essence of onion, or garlic, or smoke, or wine, or cognac. Or being machine-gunned with bits of bacon, or ham, or shrimp, or pineapple. But that usually happens to cheese already processed beyond recognition. Canning is the special horror reserved for the royalty among cheese. Ignore it.

What we do mean is that dainty and slender moon from

southeast of Paris. We mean classic Brie, the Brie whose last name is de Meaux. This is the largest and thinnest variety, running up to a foot in diameter, yet only three quarters of an inch thick. The three pretenders, Brie de Melun, Brie de Coulommiers, and Brie de Provins, are always thicker, smaller, and lacking in refinement, often being saltier and more coarsely flavored than the real thing.

Properly ripened Brie de Meaux is hard to come by— fewer than one in ten meets the standard. Look for Brie between October and April; December and March are the optimum months. After you spot an authentic wedge, check the sides. If the cheese is oozing, spilling, and otherwise vacating its rind so that the top crust is sagging, it's probably a touch overripe. Next scrutinize the inside. Beware a white caky center: the layered look, no matter how soft the part next to the rind, betrays an immature cheese. Unfortunately, once the cheese has been cut, that under-developed center can never ripen. (Some claim to have had success by covering the cheese with a damp cloth and letting it rest in a dark corner.)

The crust of a perfect Brie will have a faintly ruddy hue with white streaks. It will be bulging a bit. Inside, the cheese will have a consistently silky texture from top to bottom and a uniform gold-yellow color. Describing the taste of the perfect Brie to the uninitiated is a hopeless task. The flavor is variously said to suggest cream, truffle, leek, mushroom, cognac, Anjou pear, and earth.

If you are buying an entire wheel of Brie, obviously you can't peer inside. A touch test for firmness is not very reliable, since refrigerated Brie (and most, alas, is refrigerated) feels solid, unless it is long gone. Even if you get a chance to test the cheese at room temp, the odds of picking right by feel are modest. The only real guarantee is a trustworthy cheese shop, one that knows when the Brie was made and how it's been stored. If you find one, let us know.

HOW TO PICK THE SEX OF YOUR CHILD

Let nature take its course, and the chances are about 51 to 49 you'll have a boy. Add a little science, and you can change the odds dramatically.

The foolproof way is pretty nasty, to say the least. Cells extracted from the placenta just a few months into pregnancy provide enough clues to discover the sex of the embryo. If you don't like the result, the fetus can be aborted, and you can try again.

Less traumatic—and less successful—techniques work by changing the likelihood of conceiving a girl or a boy. Sperm carry crucial genetic information which determines the sex of the kid. Should sperm with a female (X) chromosome, rather than a male (Y) chromosome, win the race to fertilize an ovum, the baby will be a girl.

Now, it turns out that male-carrying sperm are faster swimmers than female carriers, but less able to withstand the rigors of a hostile environment. Some scientists claim that a mild vinegar (acid) douche before intercourse will improve the chances of having a girl, while a baking-soda (alkaline) douche will favor the conception of a boy. The acid douche cripples sperm of both sexes, but gives the edge to the hardier female carriers. An alkaline environment

allows the naturally speedier male sperm to win the race. This idea is forty years old, and no one has been able to prove it works, so don't count on success.

What does help for sure is timing intercourse to give male sperm an unfair advantage. Immediately after ovulation the egg is higher in the Fallopian tube, far from intruding sperm. Since male sperm move faster, the longer the distance sperm must swim, the more likely the male variety will get there first. The problem here is, of course, keeping track of when ovulation takes place. Even if you succeed, results are not guaranteed.

Methods calculated to lengthen the odds further are still experimental. Male sperm will cross a thick, liquid albumin barrier more quickly than females. Hence putting a crowd of sperm through their paces a few times in an albumin solution eliminates most of the female type. Researchers have also discovered that male- and female-carrying sperm "look different" to certain antibodies in the bloodstream. Specialized antibodies from mouse blood, for example, will attack male-carrying sperm, but ignore the female carriers. By soaking mouse sperm in an antibody-rich solution, most of the males are destroyed. Mice impregnated with the treated sperm produce six females for every four males. It's expected, too, that other antibodies will be found that knock off the female-carrying variety.

Neither method of sex selection has been tried yet on humans, so the returns aren't really in. Skeptics argue that both mechanical and chemical means of separating sperm may weaken the survivors, raising concern that the children will be born with defects. As a practical matter, it is also unlikely that many prospective parents would accept the bother of artificial insemination just to raise the odds of having a girl or a boy.

In spite of all the current difficulty, it seems probable that safe, effective sex choice is just around the corner. That may be good news for unreconstructed sorts like the Shah of Iran, but what about the rest of us? Most people want boys, or so surveys report. If parents were to have their way, things might get pretty monotonous.

HOW TO PITCH TO HENRY AARON

Why a salary-conscious veteran would ever pitch to Bad Henry, rather than pitch around him—that's the real question. Nevertheless, with the bases loaded, F.O.B. (Full of Braves or Brewers), conventional baseball wisdom decrees it moronic to walk in the run, especially with a Mathews on deck and an Adcock in the hole.

A right-handed thrower should be on the mound; keeping a southpaw in the game reduces your percentages. Preferably, the pitcher should have a herky-jerky motion like Luis Tiant. He should come from the side or, at very least, three quarters rather than from the top. Still, no one has ever accused Aaron of bailing out.

Being the premier fastball hitter—ask Drysdale—Aaron must be fed a steady diet of junk. Slow curves, change-ups, and occasionally a hard slider. Water or Vaseline also helps. Work the corners, keeping the ball low in the strike zone, never around the letters. While Aaron hits well to all fields, recently he has become a notorious pull hitter. Despite those quick wrists, keep the ball on the outside corner. Do not get behind on the count. At 2–0 or 3–1 Aaron will guess fastball, still most pitchers' safety pitch. Since his initial blast off Vic Raschi in 1951, Aaron has guessed right more than 714 times.

HOW TO PREDICT EARTHQUAKES

One minute, sometime in the next fifty years, pent-up stresses in the crust of the earth somewhere in California will cause the ground to rupture and slip a few yards. Virtually every bridge, house, road, telephone cable, and pipeline along the path of the fault will be destroyed. For miles on either side, the shock wave from the movement of trillions of tons of rock will topple poorly designed structures, crack dams and reservoirs, cut off supplies of electricity and gas and drinking water.

If there is no warning, and the fault runs through the densely populated San Francisco Bay area or through the Los Angeles sprawl, thousands, perhaps tens of thousands, will be caught in collapsing buildings or trapped by flash floods. Fires will burn out of control for hours, even days, until waterlines are restored. The shock shouldn't set any world records—perhaps three quarters of a million died in a sixteenth-century quake in China, 143,000 were killed by the Japanese Kwanto plain earthquake in 1923—but it could retire a lot of domestic trophies. The San Francisco earthquake of 1906 offed just 450 people, while the massive Alaska earthquake in 1964 killed 131.

With luck, there will be warning. Russian and American geophysicists have already pieced together some B+ reliable tests for predicting quakes days or weeks in advance, and are working on ways of forecasting big jolts as much as ten years ahead. In the months preceding a major seismic movement, stress builds up along the fault. At first, the rock is sufficiently elastic to absorb the strain. Then small cracks spread through the crust, finally followed by the slip.

The cracks provide the clues of where and when and how big. They change the electrical resistance of the rock, as well as the velocity of sound waves transmitted between points on the affected portion of the crust. The cracked rock is also more porous, allowing more water to filter through into deep underground reservoirs, and taking with it more dissolved, short-lived, radioactive gas. Hence the radioactivity of the water in deep wells increases as an earthquake approaches.

Since the late 1960's, about ten tremors have been predicted using techniques to check for cracks. Another twenty or thirty could have been predicted if anyone had bothered to monitor the earth's vital signs.

Your really big earthquakes may be detectable years in advance via still another technique. As stress builds up in the crust, it yields a bit, changing the tilt of the ground ever so slightly. Tilting was measured for ten years before a heavy quake near Niigata, Japan, in 1964. Thus sampling the tilt every few years in a few hundred sites scattered through each tremor-prone region might provide enough warning to redesign whole communities.

In spite of the obvious payoff, cash to pay for earthquake research and monitoring is very scarce—apparently it is hard to get excited about natural disasters that always seem to happen in Peru or Turkey. Maybe we'll be fortunate enough to suffer a quake somewhere out of harm's way, something big enough to scare the bureaucrats. Maybe not. Meanwhile, taxpayers in the Berkeley hills, keep your bags packed. . . .

HOW TO RATE AN OBIT IN THE NEW YORK TIMES

There are lots of ways to measure status—membership in the Century Club, a permanent suite at Claridges, a secretary for your secretary, perhaps. But the only sure way to know when you have arrived is to read what *The New York Times* says when you depart. Since none of us will have the opportunity, we offer the next-best thing, a scientific analysis of who used to be who.

Ten to fifteen souls rate an inch or more of space in the *Times* on an average day, perhaps an extra five in the Sunday edition. Of these, only one to two command a real biography and a double-column headline. While the short notices are mostly locals—former assistant Kings County district attorneys, prominent patrons of the arts in Westchester—your six-paragraph (picture optional) types aren't particularly biased in favor of New Yorkers. We checked a random sample from five years, all the obits at least eight column inches long printed in the *Times* during the third week of January of each year, to obtain the following results:

—Show biz does best, with eight of the total of sixty entries. Thereafter, it's a horse race, with politicians, businesspeople, clergy, and writers pulling down five notices each. Journalists and publishers rank next with four, followed by artists (three), scientists (three), civil servants (three), educators (three), college professors (three), diplomats (two), and a miscellaneous bunch of architects, judges, kings, foundation directors, farmers, and labor-union officials.

—To die young is to die anonymously. Only three of the sixty were under fifty years of age. Nine were over eighty-five, with the average a good seventy-four years.

—Women don't do things very often that interest *The New York Times*. Ninety percent of the obits were for men. There is no particular trend over the five years, but then not many liberated women have had a chance to die yet.

One last clue: it helps to have a famous relative. Our short list contains one Guggenheim, one Hearst, one Casadesus, and the widow of Stefan Zweig.

HOW TO READ YOUR FBI FILE

The Freedom of Information Act requires federal agencies to make public all internal documents, unless there is a good reason to keep them secret. That doesn't mean the FBI has to reveal whether they know you grow pot in the backyard. But it has been interpreted to mean the Feds owe you an accounting of all the innocent dope they've squirreled away.

Just write Clarence Kelley, Director, Federal Bureau of Investigation, Washington, D.C. 20535, the following letter:

"Pursuant to the Freedom of Information Act, Title 5, United States Code, Section 552, I hereby request access to . . ."

Describe as specifically as possible the information you want, naming dates, locations, employers, organizations, etc. The agency may ask for more details—the whole process can take months—but eventually you will see how the FBI spends its annual tithe from Congress.

HOW TO REDUCE TRAFFIC ACCIDENTS

To combat road mishaps in Peking during the 1920's, officials tried a unique approach. Drivers caught ignoring red lights at busy intersections were executed, and their heads displayed in baskets next to the traffic signals.

It worked.

HOW TO RETIRE ON $500 A MONTH

Believe it or not, there are still places in the world where $500 a month is sufficient to live well, if unluxuriously. The trick is finding one that welcomes Americans and can ac-

commodate their life style. Some of the nicest countries—
Tahiti, for example—have decided to save Paradise for the
natives, while others can't offer foreigners amenities such
as modern medical care or reasonable public sanitation.

Additional considerations: U.S. citizens living abroad
must pay taxes on income earned in the United States. This
means you may have to pay taxes twice—once to Uncle
Sam and once in your retirement country. Some places have
negligible income taxes, however, or have reciprocal agree-
ments with the United States to fleece you just one time
around. The IRS publishes a *Tax Guide for U.S. Citizens
Abroad* which lays out the alternatives.

Language can be an equally difficult hurdle. Should you
move to a country (or a region of a country) that sees few
English speakers, the going can be tough. Many—probably
most—cheap retirement spots fall in this category.

Roughing it. One of the pleasantest spots to disappear
to at any price is Greece. The cost of living (in dollars) is
as low there as anywhere in Europe. After the initial ex-
pense ($10,000) of a simple house, $400 to $500 a month
should suffice for suburban life near Athens. Move to the
Greek islands, and housing, food, and service costs decline
dramatically, but middle-class living is hardly possible.
Telephones, cars, and electricity are expensive or unavail-
able. Nowhere outside Athens are you likely to find English
speakers. The 20,000 U.S. citizens living there today are
largely returned Greek-born, first-generation Americans.

Portugal and Ireland, two other popular destinations, are
difficult for people on very limited incomes. Medical care
is inexpensive in both, but housing, transportation, and food

124

can be steep. The trick to beating high prices is to live in small towns, away from the modern world. If you can deal with the isolation, life can be very comfortable.

The big disadvantage to Ireland, of course, is the weather. The mild, western portion of the island is perpetually cloudy and damp, while the dryer (not dry) east has 60-degree summers and 40-degree winters. For Portugal, the big problems are politics and language. How welcome you will be, or how long you will remain welcome, is unclear. Few Americans can complain, though, about the attitude of the Portuguese they see each day on the street or in shops.

Living well. Tens of thousands of Americans live in Mexico, most in expatriate colonies in the big cities. The days of the Cuernavaca villa with three servants on $200 a month are long gone, but the compromises needed to live modestly on $500 a month are still small. If you do not wish to rough it in a fishing village, the best bet is Guadalajara. Lots of Americans to keep you company, low-priced apartments with standard conveniences. Mexico City and the great resort areas also have American colonies, but housing costs are unacceptably high. Mexico is fairly casual about permitting foreigners to bring in automobiles, duty free. Gasoline is a veritable steal.

Morocco also caters well to American tastes on a budget. Most of the country is incredibly poor and underdeveloped. Big exceptions are the cities booming with tourism and the new phosphate export wealth. Tangier is probably the best place for retirees. It has a large quarter populated by Europeans and Americans, sophisticated urban living, and modern housing. Moroccan cuisine is varied and delicious. Best of all, Spain is just a ferry ride away across the Strait of Gibraltar.

If you don't mind going a long, long way, New Zealand could meet your needs. The place is very quiet, very conservative; pure nineteenth-century provincial England, plus scenery. It helps to be fond of sheep. Housing, food, and medical care are substantially less than in the States. Perhaps even more important, luxuries are not missed because no one seems to have any. Climate can be a drawback; the colder of the two big islands has long winters.

The ethnic route. Many Eastern European countries—Yugoslavia, Poland, Hungary—officially welcome apolitical, first-generation Americans who want to return home to retire. Depending upon how much you and your dollars are wanted, the economics of the arrangement can be very attractive—virtually free housing and medical care (like everyone else), special access to Western luxuries in exchange for Western currencies. The drawback, naturally, is the uncertain status of non-Communist foreigners. Privileged guests today may find themselves unprivileged tomorrow. Such a move should be carefully researched, first with a visit to the foreign consulate in the United States, then with a trip abroad to talk to resident Americans and U.S. consulate bureaucrats.

HOW TO SELECT A MUTUAL FUND

SIf you are an ordinary investor, things haven't been going well for a long time. The total return (dividends plus price changes) on Standard & Poor's 500-stock average has hardly kept pace with consumer prices. Savings accounts and government bonds have been paying negative real interest (the nominal rate, less the rate of inflation) ever since LBJ decided to finance Vietnam with budget deficits. Other fixed dollar securities —industrial and municipal bonds, prime-quality commercial leases—have done O.K., but only if you were lucky enough to buy in after interest rates shot up. Commercial real estate has been a bust—a literal bust for thousands of ventures trapped between 12 percent mortgages and the nastiest recession in memory. Many homeowners can show a tidy paper profit over the last decade, thanks to explosive increases in building costs. Few, however, have been able to realize the gain in tight money markets.

Wall Street blues have also affected the mutual funds, and for good reason. Investors who thought they were paying for smart management to get them through hard times found that, in general, they were getting less than nothing for their money. The funds, over-all, did much worse than the market from 1969 through 1974. Only one fund in fifteen has managed to stay abreast of the S & P 500 in that period; luck rather than skill probably explains the one in fifteen. All this should come as no surprise to the well-informed. A study published in 1969 revealed that mutuals hadn't kept pace with the market in the 1945–64 period, either.

Why then buy a mutual fund today? It doesn't make sense for anyone with a lot of money or a lot of interest in the market. Such investors can purchase the minimal services offered by mutuals for less elsewhere, or have fun doing it themselves. If you have less than $50,000 to play with, and get no kick from the game, the funds may still be the least unacceptable among bad alternatives. Some considerations:

Specialization vs. diversification. Specialty funds specialize, concentrating their investments in gold stocks or foreign stocks or even commodity futures. A few of them have made lots of bananas—the Japan Fund, which buys only Japanese securities, has yielded nearly 20 percent annually over the decade.

If you have great faith in the future of gold mines or foreign stock exchanges or something else, specialty funds might save you some effort. In general, though, the best part of mutuals is their ability to spread your eggs among many baskets. More funds are diversifying beyond the stock market, trading bonds as well. There is no way to get rich with a diversified fund, but the chances of getting poor with one are reduced.

Growth vs. income. Most funds promise rapid growth or high income (some deliver neither). On the assumption you can find mutual funds that can do one or the other, which way to go should depend upon your objectives. Income funds try to generate big dividends, meaning you get cash each quarter (which is nice) and pay ordinary income taxes on same (which is not nice). Some income funds these days buy only bonds, or even only municipal bonds. The big theoretical advantage of the income funds is they fluctuate in value less than growth funds. This follows because dividends and bond-coupon income fluctuate less than retained corporate profits, the engine of stock growth.

Reality doesn't always follow theory, however. Some income funds hitch rides on the same roller coaster that the growth funds built. One way to beat the problem is to buy "unit trust" bond funds from a broker. Investors can suffer capital gains and losses on unit trusts as interest rates change, but there is no management to screw them up by churning the portfolio. Unit trusts stick with the initial portfolio until the bonds mature, or until all the investors redeem their shares.

Load vs. no-load. Some funds charge an initial fee, up to 8.75 percent, just to buy in. These load funds use the fee to pay their own sales force or to reward brokerage houses that do the job for them. No-loads have no sales force, relying on direct sales to the public.

There is not a reason in the world to fork over a loading fee—the load funds do no better on average than the no-loads. True, if you hold the shares for ten or twenty years, the 8 percent may not seem like much in comparison with the total return per share. But remember the interest you might have collected all those years on the money kept by the fund.

Open-end vs. closed-end. Most funds are "open-ended" —they stand ready to buy back your shares at their market value, which is a convenience. Closed-end fund shares are traded on the exchanges or over-the-counter. You buy and sell them like any stock, paying only regular trading commissions. Closed-end funds (in theory) have the advantage of giving managers a fixed amount of assets to work with. By contrast, open-end funds must remain sufficiently liquid to buy back their own shares. More serious, the open-end funds often find themselves without resources to buy precisely when the market has the most bargains. The public almost never catches a bull market until it's almost over. When the market boom is well on its way to being done, cash floods in from new investors, and managers feel compelled to buy something, though everything is overpriced.

Hence closed-end funds hold a small edge over open-enders. Remember, however, that no law requires closed-end shares to trade for the market value of the stocks behind them. Some closed-end shares sell at a premium, others at a discount. A public change in heart about the quality of your fund's management can change the value of your investment, a layer of risk that doesn't exist for open-end funds.

One possible investment strategy: buy discounted closed-end shares. If it's really true that luck determines differences in the year-to-year success of the funds, the discounted ones should have a better than even chance of outperforming the rest of the field.

Management fees. If mutual funds can't beat the market, it certainly pays to pick a fund whose managers understand the grim realities. A typical fund turns over 30 percent of its portfolio each year, costing shareholders about 1 percent of their assets. Some funds actually burn 4 or 5 percent of their capital each year, churning their way through endless expense-account lunches at Fraunces

Tavern and myriad junkets to see Synergistic Microchip, Inc.'s new Venezuelan assembly plant.

Other things equal, far better to pick a big fund with an unambitious research program and commensurately low costs. The few funds charging below 0.5 percent actually have better performance rankings than average. By this logic, the ultimate fund is an index fund, one which makes no attempt whatsoever to outscore the market. It simply uses collective purchasing power to reduce risk. Unfortunately, the only index funds around work exclusively for big bank trust departments and pension funds. Among the hundreds of funds catering to individuals, not one is willing to admit it can't beat the odds.

HOW TO SET A WORLD RECORD

Not all of us can win a Nobel prize or make a million dollars or go to a dinner party with Truman Capote. But that is no reason to live out your existence in anonymity. Thousands of world records are waiting to be set, some of which require little endurance, less strength, and no intelligence.

What is required, however, is a little ingenuity. A record is not a record unless it has style. Being on time for your dentist appointment 63 times straight doesn't count. Nor does running out of gas on the New Jersey Turnpike three weekends in a row, or listening attentively to Eric Sevareid discussing NATO troop withdrawals for more than a minute.

The best source of inspiration is, of course, the *Guinness*

Book of World Records. If you have plenty of time and money, you might try to better Mrs. Clara MacBeth's 17 solid years on a cruise ship (the S.S. *Caronia*). A cheaper and less time-consuming goal might be the world's auto-

mobile-cramming record, currently held by the Glendale Secondary School in Hamilton, Ontario. The only difficulty here is that you will need 111 friends to help. Personally, we would prefer to see somebody take a crack at the egg-

catching (intact) record, most recently set by Craig Finley of Missouri. It's not just anyone who will get in the way of an egg thrown 316 feet, 5¾ inches.

To register your world record, send all the details of the feat to the editors of the *Guinness Book of World Records:*

Main Editorial Office

2 Cecil Court

London Road, Enfield

Middlesex, England

Proof is, of course, a problem. You wouldn't just take the word of a person who claimed to catch an egg thrown 317 feet, after all. The Guinness editors ask for notarized affidavits from witnesses and, if possible, a published newspaper account.

HOW TO SKI 365 DAYS A YEAR

Sure, you do the weekend thing at Sugerbush or Tahoe. Maybe even play hooky from the office every other Wednesday in February and fight the teen-agers for possession of one of the suburban ice hills around New York or Boston or San Francisco. But if you are really serious about skiing, if you can't sleep nights wondering where the fresh-powder god spends his or her summers, we have the dope for you.

Thanksgiving–March. Who needs advice on winter skiing? Still, some places are better than others. The first East Coast mountains with reasonable natural coverage— typically, the second week in December—are Killington,

Stowe, and the big hills in Québec. Some years, though, it hardly snows at all before the weather turns windy, cold, and gray. Then your best bets are mountains with southern exposures and plenty of snowmaking equipment. Bromley in Vermont is justly famous for turning glaciers into ice cubes and ice cubes into hardpack. Mount Snow has two covered lifts to make the ascent at least bearable. For a change, try Beech Mountain or Sugar Mountain in North Carolina. These respectable hills never get very cold, yet manage to manufacture a lot of white stuff during January and February.

Out West, of course, there is no need to play games to find fluffy straight through the winter. For variety and good living the sentimental favorite is Sun Valley, though cool reason would point to Aspen. Jackson Hole, the giant of the American Rockies, is too cold to enjoy until March.

While we are at it, there is no denying the glories of mid-winter skiing in the Alps. The scenery and comforts run A+, the snow A—, and the lift lines B—. Austrian resorts (Lech, Kitzbühel, St. Anton) provide the best value; the Swiss (Zermatt, St. Moritz, Davos), singular comfort and variety; the French (Chamonix, Val d'Isère, Courchevel), chic, challenge, and food.

April–June. Decent skiing lasts well into May in the Rockies, though the character changes. Gone is the feathery powder, replaced by eminently skiable hardpack in the morning, melting corn by early afternoon. The last best powder of the spring season is usually to be had in Utah at Snowbird or Alta. Up North in British Columbia, however, the good snow sometimes remains until June. Whistler

Mountain, with 4,300 vertical feet, offers the closest facsimile to lift-served summer skiing in North America.

In Europe, the choices are narrowing rapidly by April. Voss, in Norway, has the charm of pleasant, late-season skiing without the (literal) headache of high altitude. In the Alps, good skiing is confined to the slopes above 6,000 feet. France has some of the nicest of these—La Plagne, Tignes, Alpe d'Huez. May and June mean glacier skiing, which, incidentally, lasts throughout the summer. The Chamonix Vallée Blanche gives you ten uninterrupted miles of white, spiced with an occasional crevice; the nearby Grands Montets snow bowl is tamer and safer. For sheer variety, late spring in Val d'Isère can't be topped.

July–November. Between July and October there is no contest. Follow the Olympic teams to Portillo, high, high in the Andes above Santiago, Chile. The snow is Alta-dry and almost too plentiful, burying the lifts on occasion. Slopes vary from easy–intermediate to impossible, averaging pretty tough. The hotel—there is only one hotel—doesn't rate comparison with accommodations at Aspen or St. Moritz, but you'll get by. All the airlines that fly to Chile sell two-week Portillo package deals.

Should the altitude bother you, the only real Latin-American alternative is Bariloche, Argentina, one thousand miles south of Buenos Aires. The skiing is open-slope style on fairly heavy, but plentiful, snow. No competition for Portillo. One last possibility: fairly spartan facilities serve the Villarrica area of Chile, 500 miles south of Santiago. The only clear virtue here is that the season lasts into November.

If you have an overweight wallet and an aversion to Latin dictators, check out the summer–fall skiing in New Zealand and Australia. The snow is fabulous in New Zealand, but for the moment it is accessible mostly by helicopter and ski-plane. Australia seems a long way to go for the California-quality skiing at Thredbo, between Melbourne and Sydney.

HOW TO SKINNY-DIP IN PEACE

Here, it all depends on what you want. Legal nudity has been around a lot longer than the sexual revolution, so the average nudist club is still strictly a family affair. No alcohol, no drugs; check your lust in the locker room, please. There's nothing wrong with a little clean living, of course, and it does avoid misunderstandings. So if you don't mind the combination church-social/outing-club atmosphere of most, the old-fashioned sunbathing clubs may be for you.

Finding them is easy, since many belong to one or more of the national nudist organizations. The biggest (and most conservative) of these, the American Sunbathing Association (810 North Mills Avenue, Orlando, Florida), will come up with a list of affiliates for the asking. Facilities tend to be spartan, in keeping with the ascetic image. Some clubs nick you for a membership fee—rarely very much, though. Singles (particularly males) are generally unwelcome, as are visitors who would rather watch than join.

Suppose volley ball and barbecues don't turn you on. What's left? Dozens of clubs and private resorts have sprung up in the last decade which cater to younger folks with fewer (or at least different) inhibitions. Many are where you'd expect to find them—California—but a surprising number can be found in the heartland.

The ambiance varies enormously, from Grossinger's-without-clothes to strictly X-rated. Dick Drost's Naked City put Rose Lawn, Indiana, on the map with annual Miss Nude World and Miss Nude Teenybopper contests. Between beauty pageants, when upright citizens of Chicago and Indianapolis aren't ogling contestants (spectators pay $15 for the privilege), Naked City keeps sun lovers busy with miniature golf, Ping-Pong, swimming, archery, sauna, and much, much more. Should you so desire, the Treehouse Fun Ranch in San Bernardino, California, will accommodate a yen to sky-dive in the buff. You must, however, wear a parachute. More typically, the new-style nude resorts are like the old-style, but without all the rules. Singles are accepted, if not encouraged. Drinking is permitted—in fact, the bar probably supports the rest of the enterprise. Swingers coexist with straights.

If you don't want to go to the trouble of finding your own place in the sun, V.I.B.* Tours (902 Second Avenue, New York, New York 10017) sells packaged vacations. Destinations include tolerant Caribbean islands and nearby beaches, as well as nude resorts.

For all this organized activity, it is still possible to find

* Figure it out for yourself.

places where you can legally take a plunge *au naturel* without joining a club, booking a tour, or entering the Nude Olympics. By far the nicest are in Europe, on Yugoslavia's Adriatic coast and on the French Riviera. Yugoslavia, eager for tourists, happily accommodates travelers who wish to alternate their days between sightseeing in the medieval city-states along the coast and purer forms of hedonism. Try the beaches on the island of Hvar, where Marshal Tito maintains a summer home, or those near Zadar.

French police permit casual, unorganized nudity to flourish on the isolated Ile du Levant, and topless sunbathers to mingle with the crowds all along the Côte d'Azur. Lately, it has become chic to show everything in St. Trôpez. One real-estate developer is building a posh nude resort farther down the Mediterranean coast near Spain, with condominiums to purchase or lease by the month. Write Club Nature Sogenat, Port Nature, 34300 Cap d'Agde, France.

Closer and cheaper, both American shorelines have their share of nude beaches. The U.S. Park Service officially claims neutrality on the subject, but in practice bans skinny-dipping on park property when enough people complain. The California coast between San Francisco and San Diego is loaded with free public beaches. Among the prettiest are Gaviota Beach north of Santa Barbara, Black's Beach in La Jolla, and San Gregorio north of Santa Cruz. Trouble is, it's hard to predict month to month where you will be safe from harassment by the police. As a rule, nudity is tolerated until it becomes too popular to ignore. Check things out ahead, unless you secretly yearn to have your name on a

Supreme Court case. On the East Coast, the best free beaches are in Massachusetts (Truro, Zach's in Martha's Vineyard) and New York (Fire Island). The same warnings apply.

A final choice for catching rays in absolute privacy: the Pavilions and Pools Hotel on St. Thomas, U.S. Virgin Islands, offers individual guest houses for two to four, each with a small pool in a walled courtyard. The maid comes only when invited.

HOW TO SPEND A WEEKEND IN NEW YORK WITHOUT LOSING YOUR SHIRT

Some people claim New York is the most expensive city in the world. Anyone who has booked a $90 double in Geneva recently or dropped $40 on a steak in Tokyo knows better. It's true that New York's famous hotels, restaurants, and theaters flaunt their expense-account goodies shamelessly —the Palace, a recently arrived French restaurant, achieved instant success by posting a $50 prix-fixe dinner. But the savvy visitor can live high without risking insolvency.

Hotels. Tourists seem aware of only two sorts, the grand deluxe hotels, like the Pierre, Plaza, Lombardy, and Regency, or the mass-production types catering to conventions, like the Hilton, Americana, and Sheraton. Yet comfortable middle-class hotels, charging $20 to $30 for double rooms, are still to be found in the heart of midtown Manhattan. The Tudor (304 East Forty-second Street), a beautifully maintained old place, lacks none of the services of the grand hostelries and has few of the security problems that plague the huge convention hotels. The Seville (22 East Twenty-ninth Street) is a bit out of the way, but makes up for it with newly remodeled rooms, including color TV. In contrast to the neighborhood, the Abbey Victoria (Seventh Avenue at Fifty-first Street) is a cheerful spot. Few of the one thousand rooms could win a decorator's award, yet they rate above average on privacy and comfort. Ask for one of the interior rooms, genuine oases of quiet in the Times Square area.

Restaurants. Since there are so many places to eat, a restaurant strategy is more important than specific recommendations. The first rule is to avoid competition with diners who hardly care what they pay—business people impressing each other on company funds, couples from Greenwich and Short Hills second-guessing the *New York Times* critic's choice of the city's best wine list.

Rule #2: Sample neighborhood ethnic restaurants specializing in Chinese, Jewish, Greek, Thai, Spanish, Rumanian, Czech, and Latin food. With French restaurants, avoid the high-rent district east of Sixth Avenue, and concentrate on country rather than haute cuisine. Some personal favorites:

• Chef Ma's (10 Pell Street). One of New York's best Chinese restaurants, though we would be nuts to claim it will remain so indefinitely. In Chinatown, chefs come and go, owners get bored or greedy, aficionados drift on. Chef Ma's makes no fetish about having the latest dishes from Hunan or Yunnan. Whatever you order, however, is likely to be good. Try beef with whole baby corn, pork with scallions, or kidneys in pepper sauce.

143

- Czechoslovak Praha (First Avenue at Seventy-third Street). Bring a big appetite. The food is pure Middle Europe, not really distinguishable from New York German. But the Praha does it better—for relatively little money—than anyone else in the city. The garlic in the Czech sausage platter will send you reeling for more Pilsner. The roast goose is matched only by the roast duck. For dessert, poppy-seed strudel is a must.

- Landmark Tavern (Eleventh Avenue at Forty-sixth Street). Far, far to the west of the theater district, the Landmark Tavern nestles amidst auto-body repair shops and condemned factories. It's worth a taxi ride, though. The bargain menu is plain American with touches of class—home-baked soda bread aromatic with spices and candied fruit, perfect cottage fries, the world's largest martini. The short wine card lists good bottles at just a dollar or two above the store price. But what's really special is the setting. The Landmark is just that, an impeccably restored nineteenth-century drinking establishment with tile floors, globe light fixtures, and a long, black, polished wood bar.

- Pierre au Tunnel (Forty-eighth Street between Eighth and Ninth Avenues). The area specializes in moderately priced French restaurants, many of which rate as good values. Our choice, Pierre au Tunnel, looks a little down at the mouth, but makes up for it with a competent, consistent kitchen. All the fresh fish are pretty good, the cold salmon with mayonnaise, outstanding. And the vegetables come nicely undercooked.

- Parkway (157 Chrystie Street). Our idea of New York's grandest stuff. A full-course dinner at the Parkway could put you on cottage cheese and melba toast for a month. The food is Jewish-Rumanian: broiled meats, chopped liver, Eastern European pastries. And where else in the United States can you find pitchers of chicken fat and seltzer dispensers on the tables along with the salt and pepper?

• Marchi's (251 East Thirty-first Street). Excellent northern Italian food for half the price of the midtown fettuccine villas. The trick is that Marchi's serves only one menu: antipasto, lasagne, fried fish, roast chicken, lemon fritters, cheese, fruit, espresso. The antipasto is simple and elegant, the lasagne a model of fresh pasta. We aren't fans of the Italian desserts, but you may be.

Movies. No one comes to New York to see first-run Hollywood flicks. Robert Redford looks the same in Seattle, and, chances are, back home the Saturday-night line will be shorter, the tickets cheaper, the popcorn hotter. What New York does have that are hard to find elsewhere are revival houses, theaters showing golden oldies and otherwise un-distributed foreign films. The Elgin (Eighth Avenue at Nineteenth Street) changes double features every second day, while the Museum of Modern Art (11 West Fifty-third Street) shows as many as 1,000 films each year. Movies at MOMA are included in the museum admission.

Less dependable revival schedules (the form flourishes only in the summer) can be found at the Bleecker Street Cinema (Greenwich Village), the Carnegie Hall Cinema (Seventh Avenue at Fifty-seventh Street), and the Quad (34 West Thirteenth Street).

Theater. Would you pay $16 to see a Broadway musical? Thousands do each week. Off-Broadway, the orchestra seats at $10 are not exactly a bargain, either. Enter the Times Square Theatre Center, a big trailer parked on the traffic island at Forty-seventh Street and Broadway. Every day starting at 3 P.M. (noon on weekends and matinee Wednesdays), the Theatre Center sells leftover Broadway and Off-Broadway tickets for half price. The big hits are rarely available, but it's a cinch to find something interesting from the dozen or so shows which have seats to fill.

Other low-cost possibilities are the Off-Off Broadway theaters. While Off-Broadway turned commercial a decade ago, experimental theater is alive and well in New York. Quality varies from awful to the best in town, with ten or fifteen productions to pick from on an average weekend. OOB is scattered all over Manhattan, with the major concentration in the Bowery area. Theaters are born (and die) every few months; the best way to find out what's happening this week is to check the "Arts and Leisure Guide" in the Sunday *Times*.

Opera. The Metropolitan Opera may or may not be the best in the country, but it certainly is the most expensive. An established alternative (for one half the price) is the New York City Opera, located just across the Lincoln Center Plaza from the Met. City productions have fewer star singers, yet are totally professional by any standard.

Opera buffs with an ear for the unusual may also be surprised by the quality of the semi-professional companies around New York, which specialize in less well known productions. Two companies connected with music schools, the American Opera Center (Juilliard) and the John

Brownlee (Manhattan), stand out from the rest. The American is more ambitious, maintaining high standards for costumes and sets as well as music. Programs and tickets for both are available from the schools.

Others worth hearing: the Amato Opera, the Bronx Opera, the New York Grand Opera, and the New York Lyric Opera. All these companies perform at infrequent intervals; check the Sunday *Times* for what's around when you're around.

Dance. For classical ballet, it pays to stick with well-known groups—the Joffrey, the New York City Ballet. Ballet needs good stages, and tickets aren't that expensive, anyway. Modern dance is another matter. New York is loaded with fine companies: established names like Martha Graham, Merce Cunningham, and Paul Taylor, but unknowns (charging almost nothing for tickets) as well. The best way to keep in touch is with the listings and reviews in the *Village Voice*.

HOW TO SPOT CROOKED DICE

Craps is the biggest moneymaker in Las Vegas, and for good reason. Casinos like it because they can't lose—in an honest game the house has an edge (up to 11 percent) on every bet accepted. Gamblers like it because the action is so fast. Fortunes can be won or lost in a few minutes. Cheats like it because the opportunities for beating the odds the easy way are almost limitless.

147

The key, of course, to cheating at craps is fixing the dice. Craps is a pure gambling game; there's no real skill involved beyond learning the jargon and scanning a probability table in *Scarne's Complete Guide to Gambling*. One player rolls the dice, and you bet on the outcome of each toss or series of tosses. The only way to win in the long run is to distort the chances of certain combinations. Some possibilities:

Flats. Shaving down one side of a die makes it larger than four of the five other sides. Even a difference as small as one five-hundredth of an inch can shift the odds noticeably, though much larger shaves are common. You should be able to spot flat dice by comparing them with a straight edge on a smooth surface.

Bevels and cut edges. If one face of a die bulges slightly in the middle, the chances of landing on that side are reduced. These are called—somewhat misleadingly— bevels. You can accomplish the same objective by sanding some of the edges of the dice at an angle greater than 45 degrees, shrinking the surface area of one side more than the adjacent sides. In both cases, the only way to catch a skillful cheat is to compare two dice. Beveled dice, side by side, wobble. For cut-edge dice, make a similar side-by-side comparison, concentrating your attention on the corners.

Casinos have a stake in preventing any variations in shapes, since they accept bets for or against the player. To guard against switches, the casino may order dice of a special size and color for easy comparison with the dice in play. In any event, dice are changed frequently.

Loaded dice. A bit of extra weight on one side of the die will make the opposite side come up more often than by

148

chance. Even transparent dice can be loaded by secreting tiny lead or gold slugs in the drilled spots, while filling the light-side spots with paint. To test for a load, hold the die in question at the top of a tall glass of water. Drop it carefully, and see if it settles to the bottom without rotating on the way down.

Tops. The crudest form of crooked dice, yet the kind favored by professional cheaters. Opposite sides on tops show the same numbers, so each die has a total of only three numbers instead of six. Since it's possible to see only three sides at once, the professional can substitute tops in play as long as no one else is able to examine them. Tops can be 100 percent winners, or percentage winners, depending on how the game is played. Using them, however, takes guts and skill. The mechanic must be prepared to substitute honest dice for tops, or switch between kinds of tops, at a moment's notice. Generally "bust-out" men operate in teams under the protection of, and with extra help provided by, local hoods. If you suspect you are being taken with tops, stop betting and move on fast. Challenging the integrity of a bust-out artist can be detrimental to the health.

HOW TO TALK BACK TO JOHN SIMON

Phone 212 MU 5–8413.
Good luck.

HOW TO TELL THE PLAYERS WITHOUT A SCORECARD

In these days of investigative journalism, when reporters must be prepared to do anything for a story, it's nice to know that some of the news still comes from official sources. For a recent Presidential fence-mending trip with NATO allies, the White House Press Corps received detailed information on the European political situation. Included was the on-the-record report that Vatican City was inhabited by Roman Catholics. Vatican spokesmen had no immediate comment.

HOW TO TELL WHEN IT'S YOUR TURN

Every person has a time and, possibly, a prime. To find out when you're due—at least according to a sociologist who looked it up—consult the chart.

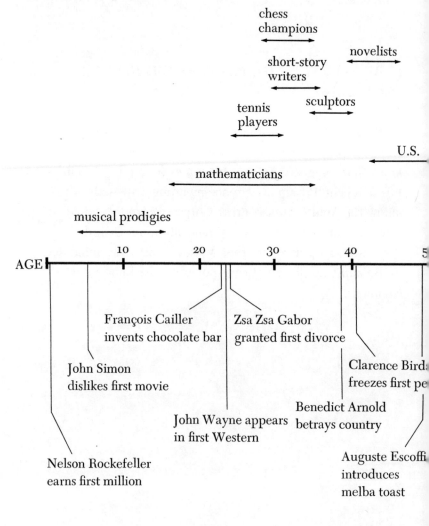

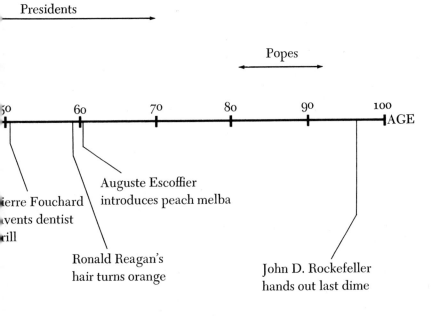

Presidents

Popes

50   60   70   80   90   100 AGE

Auguste Escoffier
introduces peach melba

ierre Fouchard
vents dentist
ill

Ronald Reagan's
hair turns orange

John D. Rockefeller
hands out last dime

HOW TO TRACE YOUR FAMILY TREE

It's not like knowing where you are going, but knowing where you came from can be a comfort. Should you get the urge, there are two ways to begin.

Do it yourself. Genealogy is mostly hard work. If you have plenty of time and are not too ambitious, a few hundred letters, a few months in libraries, and a few trips to Washington should be sufficient. The place to start, of course, is personal family records—old letters, diaries, Bibles. For American genealogy, 1880 is the watershed. State and local records (registrations of births, deaths, marriages, divorces, wills) are reasonably accurate and complete since that date, but of much less value for earlier years.

If you know your ancestors arrived in the United States before 1880, it makes sense to look first in the National Archives. They contain vast quantities of nineteenth-century records: manuscripts of the U.S. Census dating back to 1790, war records, naturalization documents, ships' passenger lists, deeds of public land sales. The *Guide to Genealogical Records in the National Archives* (order it for 65 cents from the U.S. Government Printing Office, Washington, D.C. 20402) provides details. To find out much, the chances are good that a personal visit to the Archives in Washington will be needed. The Archives' staff is prepared, though, to process some requests by mail.

Other sources provide specialized information. The DAR maintains more than 200,000 files on members' lineage, which, naturally, date back to the Revolution. Military draft

records from World War I can be obtained from the Federal Records Center in East Point, Georgia. The genealogical collection amassed by the Mormon Church, largely based on hard-to-find state and local records, is open to the public in Salt Lake City, Utah. Old newspaper indices are of limited value, with the notable exception of the *Boston Evening Transcript* for the years 1876–1923. The *Transcript* and others are preserved by the Library of Congress in Washington.

The compleat genealogist must learn to be suspicious. Beware of collections of biographical sketches and photographs contributed by subscribers. These "mug" books stuff the shelves of every genealogical library, and although some are accurate, more are self-serving or carelessly compiled. Note, too, the casual name spelling and descriptions of family relationships in nineteenth-century sources. Brother, for example, can mean brother-in-law, stepbrother, or even fellow church member. For records before 1752, dates can also be confusing. Often two dates, the Gregorian and the unreformed, are cited. If you get this far, invest in one of the handbooks for amateur genealogists. Gilbert Doane's *Searching for Your Ancestors* (University of Minnesota Press) is first-rate.

Hire a pro. Answer one of those little ads in the back of a magazine, and you are likely to get a few made-up paragraphs on the origin of your name, assurances you are descended from Charlemagne, and a bill for $200. Reliable genealogists advertise rarely, except in trade publications like the *American Genealogist*, the *New England Historical and Genealogical Register*, and the *New York Genealogical and Biographical Record*. The Board for the Certification of Genealogists (1307 New Hampshire Avenue, N.W., Washington, D.C. 20036) keeps lists of reliable professionals, broken down by specialty.

Expect to pay $10 to $25 per hour for the service, with a minimum of $300 to $500. Should you get very serious, the final bill can end up ten times that high. Tracing ancestry back to Europe is particularly expensive. Remember, it's cricket to shop around for estimates and compare prices.

HOW TO TURN A FAST BUCK

Let's first write off the romantic scenarios. Sure, it would be great to invent a car that runs on potato peelings, or peddle your kid's grade-school watercolors as genuine American primitives, or jump the Mississippi on a motorcycle for ABC–TV. Great, but it's just not likely to happen.

For every fortune acquired making something, ten are based on speculation. Mostly, speculators operate on luck, or on the stupidity of other speculators. We herewith offer a short primer on how not to be stupid—you'll have to supply your own luck.

First principles. It's easy to make a lot of money if you already have a lot of money. Well, if not easy, at least easier. The alternative to starting with a fat wallet is leverage, making ordinary investments inordinately risky. Suppose you buy one Picasso oil for $50,000. If it appreciates 10 percent, you've made $5,000; if it depreciates 10 percent, you've lost $5,000. Suppose, instead, you buy ten Picasso oils on credit at $50,000 each, with just a $50,000 down payment. Now if the paintings appreciate 10 percent, you've made an extra $50,000. If they depreciate 10 percent, you've lost your shirt.

Along with leverage, the ambitious speculator must find ways to trade with low transaction costs. Buy a hundred shares of Ma Bell at 50, then sell them two weeks later at 52. You've made $200, right? Wrong. Merrill Lynch will probably keep the first $150 as a souvenir. Worst yet, try buying and selling a piece of land in Florida. Chances are, the brokers and lawyers will walk away with 10 or 20 percent of the cash, whether or not the deal turns a profit.

157

A good speculator must also pick a game in which it is possible to become an expert. There is no way to become an expert at roulette, hence no one to be smarter than. The most tantalizing speculations are those in which expertise helps (and can be acquired without special connections), yet which somehow still attract non-experts. Professional speculators spend much of their energy searching out the dummies.

Warrants. Once upon a time, before the Great Crash (we mean the 1929 one), the hottest game in town was the stock market. Speculating in stocks was easy because brokerage houses were happy to lend money to customers, provided they left the securities as collateral. During the Depression, once the smoke had cleared, the mean old Federal Reserve Board put a stop to these easy-credit policies by imposing margin requirements. Now you can't borrow more than half the value of the stock you buy.

Enter the warrant. A warrant is a certificate entitling the owner to buy stock direct from the company at a specified price. Say Chrysler issues a warrant to buy the stock for 10 when it is trading at 11. That makes the warrant worth a dollar. Now consider the alternatives. If you buy $1,100 worth of the stock, and Chrysler goes from 11 to 15, you make a profit of just $400 (less commissions). But suppose instead you spend the $1,100 on 1,100 warrants at a dollar each. When the stock hits 15, each Chrysler warrant will be worth at least 5, and you'll have a profit of $4,400. That's leverage, whether the Federal Reserve likes it or not.

PROGNOSIS: Warrants with fixed time limits were once almost routinely tossed in as a sweetener in new stock issues ("Buy one hundred shares of Kentucky Fried Matzo and receive without-obligation-at-no-extra-cost six warrants to purchase KFM at 10"). Fewer warrants are floating around these days, and fewer people are trading them, so the market is smaller and thinner. Big investment and brokerage houses can and do influence warrant values, especially near their expiration date. Hence this is no place for smart action. There are too many pros around, ready to eat you for breakfast.

Options. If you like the idea of warrants—betting that a stock will go up without actually having to buy it—you'll like options even better. A call option is a private contract between potential buyer and seller. The seller, in exchange for cash now, agrees to deliver stock at a fixed price anytime over the life of the option. If IBM is selling at 200, the option to buy a share tomorrow for 180 is worth $20. The option to buy IBM anytime over the next six months for 180 may be worth twice that much or more, depending on IBM's prospects and the general volatility of the stock market.

The super advantage of option buying is leverage. A staid old blue chip can be turned into a speculator's dream via the option—an increase or decrease in stock value of only a few percentage points will typically be magnified tenfold in the option. Until a few years ago, the problem with options was the cost of getting in and out. Option buyers and sellers were matched up individually by brokers, who charged fat fees for their services. To add to the speculator's woes, the only way to cash in on good fortune was to exercise the option, collect the stock, and pay yet another commission to sell the shares.

Now both the Chicago Board Options Exchange and the

American Stock Exchange make markets for call options. This has lowered option purchase commissions and eliminated the need to exercise the option to realize a profit. The option itself can be resold on the exchange.

PROGNOSIS: If speculation is what you want, this is probably the place to be. Insiders are unlikely to manipulate prices since option values are (loosely) tied to stock values. The market is enormous, meaning that buying and selling is cheap and simple. The real problem with options is the speed of the track. Option buying is one of the fastest ways to build a fortune—that's great, but only if you can afford to absorb the possible losses.

Foreign currency. Along with speculating on the fortunes of common stocks, it's also possible to bet on the exchange rate between national currencies. The language of foreign-exchange speculation is less familiar to amateurs, but the mechanics are pretty much the same. First and simplest, you can just buy foreign currency with dollars at your bank—British pounds, Swiss francs, and German marks are all popular—then repurchase U.S. currency after its price has fallen—that is, after the dollar has depreciated vis-à-vis other currencies. Depending on the size of the transaction, round-trip commissions will be 0.5 to 2 percent. This isn't a very risky operation, but the chances of big profits are slim. Major currencies rarely fluctuate more than 10 percent per year against the dollar.

There are two easy ways to goose up the leverage in foreign-exchange speculation. First, you can buy or sell forward contracts, specific obligations to deliver or accept foreign currencies at a given exchange rate a month or more in the future. The American Board of Trade in New

York requires just 10 percent down on standard contract units of about $2,500. Better still, the International Monetary Market in Chicago allows margin deposits of just 2–5 percent (depending on the activity of the currency). It's possible—even probable—that you will double your investment or lose it all within a few weeks. Both exchanges, incidentally, charge very low commissions.

The alternative to trading forward contracts is to buy options on foreign currencies. Foreign-currency options are just what they sound like. They offer one faint advantage over forward contracts—no transaction need take place at the end of the contract period.

PROGNOSIS: Trouble all the way. The foreign-exchange markets are dominated by multinational corporations, very large banks, oil barons, and worried governments. Do you really want to bet on what Sheik Yamani will think next month about the safety of the British pound? Remember the fate of the Franklin National Bank. Moreover, the forward market for us small fry (and in this game a small fry is anyone who invests less than $1,000,000 a shot) is very thin. You may find yourself ready to sell those Canadian-dollar contracts and have no one to sell them to. Leave this one for the gnomes in Zurich. Unless you know what they are thinking, currency speculation amounts to shooting craps. (See "How to Spot Crooked Dice.")

Commodities futures. The oldest and one of the heaviest trips around. Almost anything that is eaten or woven or burned or hoarded has a futures market these days—cotton, potatoes, orange juice, pork bellies, coffee, soybeans, crude-oil tankers, propane gas, plywood, coconut oil, turkeys—you name it. Any stockbroker will be happy to help you drop a few thousand getting a feel for commodities; there's really nothing to it. Ponder the advantages: Commissions are low and leverage can be spectacular. Only a few hundred dollars' margin entitles you to follow the fortunes of 50,000 pounds of potatoes, 2.7 million eggs, 500 bales of cotton, or 15,000 pounds of frozen orange-juice concentrate.

PROGNOSIS: The chances of an even break are fair, provided you stay with heavily traded commodities. Futures prices are determined both by real market forces (Will the red-winged bat fly decimate the Illinois soybean crop? Will the tea drinkers of London switch to Nescafé freeze-dried?) and by the manipulation of major speculators. It's best to stick with markets that are too large to be controllable by a few traders and sufficiently comprehensible to outsiders to give you a fighting chance. The modest size of the potato, flaxseed, mercury, and various petroleum-product markets disqualifies them as places for a neophyte. The scarcity of public information about cattle hides, wheat, and most industrial metals gives too much of an edge to insiders.

This still leaves some markets which can make you a million overnight—coffee, cocoa, sugar, coconut oil, pork bellies, soybeans. If you had purchased one six-month, 5,000-bushel soybean future ($1,000 margin) early in 1973, you would have multiplied your investment thirty times by summer. Buy a sugar future now ($2,500 margin) and every time the price goes up a nickel a pound, you've made $5,600.

Virtually every brokerage house or investment service offers a system for staying ahead in commodities trading—the same system. Simply cut your losses and let your profits ride. If you lose half your margin deposit, sell out. But don't sell on the upside until you have at least tripled your cash.

We are very skeptical. Like any system, it can work only if few people understand what is going on. And far too many know about this one. The only thing anyone knows for sure about commodities is that there are more losers than winners. According to a Securities and Exchange Commission survey, three out of four speculators end up with less than they started.

Gold. Thanks to congressional benevolence, Americans now have the chance to imitate Indian shopkeepers, French peasants, and Arab billionaires by hoarding gold bullion. Of course, it was always possible to own gold—directly as coins, jewelry, nuggets, and the like, or indirectly as mining stocks. But it's just not the same as collecting those pretty little $10,000 paperweight-size bricks.

Buying and selling couldn't be easier. Most large banks function as brokers. They will also store and insure the stuff (for a fee) or rent you a safe-deposit box. A couple of new mutual funds will also perform the service. One serious snag here is the problem of avoiding local sales taxes, which can raise total transaction costs to 10 percent of the purchase price in some states. A gold futures market also exists, permitting tons of leverage and cutting the cost of getting in and out in a hurry.

PROGNOSIS: Strictly for suckers, the kind of people who pay $1,000 a year for newsletters describing the ever-imminent demise of capitalism. As assorted experts with Eastern European accents and thin lips explain to their clients, gold tends to appreciate vis-à-vis paper currencies due to inflation. That is an excellent reason not to put your savings into 100,000-lira notes, though hardly a reason to cast your lot with the gold bugs. Investing in gold metal means storage costs and forgone interest, not to mention the risk of not so rare variations in gold prices. Coins and jewelry are even worse, since only a part of their value is tied to gold content.

Gold-mine stocks and gold futures are somewhat more interesting, since both involve substantial leverage. Modest increases in the price of gold may open up lower-grade mining reserves, doubling or tripling the profits of the owners. We still don't think this is a place for smart people. Gold prices rise and fall at the assorted whims of a bunch of nuts.

V HOW TO VANQUISH THE SOMMELIER

You are at La Caravelle or Chasen's, perhaps Maxim's in Chicago or La Bourgogne in San Francisco. A $21 Puligny-Montrachet '72 has been chilled, the cork removed. The wine waiter carefully pours a half inch into your glass. A moment to savor the bouquet, a tiny sip, a thoughtful pause. A nod to the waiter, and your guests' glasses are filled; the ritual is complete. Right?

Wrong. If you are going to spend $21 for a six-dollar bottle of Puligny-Montrachet, do it the French way. The purpose of a sommelier is to help you select an appropriate wine, and then protect you from the occasional spoiled bottle. After the bottle has been opened, an experienced sommelier should be able to tell if the wine is right from the smell of the cork. If he/she is not certain, a small amount is then tasted—by the sommelier. By the time the wine reaches your glass, all doubts should be resolved.

Now, a real sommelier knows this. The tasting charade is only a concession to popular expectations. If you have reason to believe the sommelier is competent, decline the offer to second-guess. If you don't have reason to believe the sommelier is competent, why are you paying $21 for that six-dollar Burgundy?

HOW TO WIN AT THE TRACK

WAmericans stake about $5 billion a year on thoroughbreds, not counting what they bet through bookies and New York OTB. About 12 percent of the total is bled off by hungry state legislatures, another 7 or 8 percent ends up in the pockets of tracks and horse owners. That still leaves $4 billion, $4 billion just waiting to be skimmed by those players who know more than the competition.

The hope and despair of gambling on horses is the pari-mutuel system. Despair because the odds are permanently and irrevocably against you. There is just no way to break the bank. Winners are more than offset by losers on every race, since just over 80 cents of every dollar wagered is returned. Hope because you are not betting against the house. Most of the money bet on races is dumb money, cash casually tossed away on whim or uncasually tossed away on addiction. To wager successfully—or, at least, lose with intelligence—consider the following:

All systems based on manipulating the size of your bet are worthless. This follows from logic, not experience. One classic "perfect" system for betting on horses mimics the classic sucker's system for roulette. Start with a two-dollar bet on your favorite horse (in roulette, read color or number). If you win, set aside your earnings, and bet two dollars again. If you lose, increase your bet on the next race, so a winning payoff will get you back even. Keep raising the ante as long as you lose, but once you win, start afresh with two dollars.

Sounds great, but there is a catch. If you lose enough times in a row, the amount needed to recoup on a single race will become enormous. Once you're broke, you're broke. (In Las Vegas, the system can be stopped before bankruptcy simply by losing enough times to reach the house limit.) True, it might take a long time to hit an unlucky streak of ten or twenty races, but meanwhile you aren't winning very much. A year of winning two dollars an hour will not compensate for losing $5,000 just once.

Subtler money-management systems don't work either. Veteran gamblers, above such superficially flawed sucker plays, show amazing faith in what is called the Dutch Book. Suppose you eliminate six of eight horses in a race, but can't decide among the remaining two. By splitting your bet between the two you are very likely to have a winner.

So far, so good. But suppose horse Number One will pay $10 to win, and Number Two just $5 to win. If you wager $2 on each, and Number One wins, you net $6; if Number Two wins you are ahead by only $1. To avoid this difference, professionals often bet smaller amounts on the horse running at longer odds. Bet $2 on Number One and $4 on Number Two, and whichever horse wins you net $4. Sounds very tidy.

It is very tidy—but that is all it is. There is no difference between Dutching two horses in each of 100 races, and *randomly* picking between the two horses in each race, then betting twice as much on the randomly chosen one.

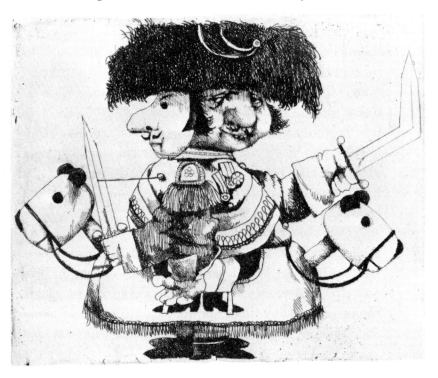

Your winnings (or losses) will be the same as long as you risk the same amount of capital. Good and bad luck will wash out in the long run.

The only way to bet is to bet to win. Race tracks have discovered that nothing draws crowds like enormous pay-offs. The old-fashioned Daily Double (picking winners in the first two races) typically pays $50, sometimes as much as $1,000. Enter the Quinella (picking the first two finishers in one race), the Exacta (picking the first two finishers in order), the Big Q (picking the first two finishers in two races), etc. They are tougher to call and generate even more fantastic results. Something named the Five-Ten at Caliente (Tijuana, Mexico) involves guessing winners in six consecutive races and can produce payoffs close to a quarter million dollars.

In theory, combinations should be promising territory for the smart bettor, since they attract so many amateurs. In practice, they are hopeless, because the necessary calculations are too difficult to make under time pressure. It's even worse for an ordinary place or show bet. While the tote board continuously recalculates the odds on win bets, there is no way to figure out ahead of time what you'll win on a place or show bet. Making a place bet is like buying a lottery ticket. Do it often enough and you are almost certain to lose 20 percent of whatever you risk.

Tout sheets work, but not well enough. Fifty cents or a buck buys you a printed set of tips at any track. These tout sheets—and newspaper predictions—are not, in general, rip-offs. People who know a fair amount about handicapping are behind them, and they typically predict better than chance. Better than chance isn't sufficient, however, unless they can also beat the one-fifth parimutuel cut. None that we know is able to do this. Tout sheets are written the day before the race, before scratches are announced, before the condition of the track is known, and before the track's tote board provides the slightest clue about odds at post time. Scratches can affect the pace of the race; rain or mud can drastically change a horse's performance; and a horse that looks like a good bet at 6–1 may end up a high-risk sentimental 5–2 favorite at the starting gate. And when a good tout does uncover a long shot that deserves a fling at 30–1, the mere mention of it in print drives the odds down to 5–1.

To win you must follow a system. We don't mean betting on the second favorite in every race, or all horses with famous jockeys. Some very simple systems doubtless put you ahead of chance, but none can even come close to beating the odds after the track eats its 20 percent. The only systems that have a chance are those based on handicapping.

Now, unless you are really into gambling (and horses), handicapping is a bore to learn and a bore to practice. Handicapping requires figuring out which characteristics matter how much and then doing the necessary calculations for each horse in each race. To learn how, start with *Ainslie's Complete Guide to Thoroughbred Racing.*

The least time-consuming way to fabricate your system is to make up ten hypothetical systems and try them all (on paper) over the course of a hundred races. If none of them produces win records that make money, try again. If you do find a winning system—and they do exist—don't make exceptions. The urge to discard hard-won information is overwhelming. But once you abandon the scientific method, the 20 percent track take will chop you into little pieces.

Remember, too, the hidden costs of gambling:

—Unless you abandon civilized society, all those hours poring over the *Daily Racing Form* must have a price.

—Any system requires a bankroll—you must be prepared to lose occasionally—so any system means lost interest at the bank. Trivia, if you risk $50 a week. Real money, if you gamble for a living.

—The Internal Revenue Service does not approve of wagering, even the legal kind. Gambling profits are taxed as regular income. Gambling losses can offset winnings, but are not otherwise deductible as business expenses. And if you use the standard deduction option on your income tax, gambling losses don't even count against gains. On big winners (any over 300–1)—Exactas, Quinellas, etc.—the IRS is tipped off by the track. For less dramatic events, paying the tax is strictly between you and the law (see "How to Choose a Federal Prison").

HOW TO . . .

ACKNOWLEDGMENTS

Thanks to Jason Bonderoff, Chris Casson, William Coury, Don Cutler, John Gerald, Charles Gerson, Mary-Joan Gerson, Janna Gordon-Elliot, Judy Green, Cynthia van Hazinga, Judy Hébert, Barbara Jackson, Peter Kornman, Meyer Kutz, Susan Lee, Beth Linebaugh, J. T. Luyt, Donna Morris, Jeffrey Morris, Barbara Neilson, Nick Passell, Winston Previant, Gideon Rosen, Richard Rigelhaupt, Leonard Ross, David Schwartz, Anthony Shafto, Don Shafto, Emily Smith, Martin Smith, Milburn Smith, Tom Stewart, Roger Straus, Dennis Thiet, Carolyn Washburne, Marilyn Wellons, Phil Wellons.

Passell, Peter
HOW TO.